P9-BYH-075

Better Homes and Gardens®

Christmas
At Home

By the Fireside

BETTER HOMES AND GARDENS® BOOKS
Des Moines, Iowa

Better Homes and Gardens®

Christmas
At Home

By the Fireside

BETTER HOMES AND GARDENS® BOOKS

An Imprint of Meredith® Books

President, Book Group: Joseph J. Ward

Vice President and Editorial Director: Elizabeth P. Rice

Executive Editor: Connie Schrader

Art Director: Ernest Shelton

Art Production Director: Randall Yontz

Test Kitchen Director: Sharon Stilwell

CHRISTMAS AT HOME: BY THE FIRESIDE

Project Director: Joni Prittie; Ceci Powell, Assistant

Editorial Project Manager: Heidi Kaisand

Graphic Designer: Irene Morris, Morris Design

Illustrations: Mike Prittie and Joni Prittie

Copy Editor: Sylvia Hauser

Proof Reader: Jennifer Mitchell

Food Stylists: Janet Pittman and Jennifer Peterson

Photographers: Batista Moon Studios and Perry Struse

Photostyling: Joni Prittie; Jodee Risney, Assistant

Meredith Corporation Corporate Officers:
Chairman of the Executive Committee: E. T. Meredith III
Chairman of the Board, President and Chief Executive Officer: Jack D. Rehm
Group Presidents: Joseph J. Ward, Books; William T. Kerr, Magazines; Philip
A. Jones, Broadcasting; Allan L. Sabbag, Real Estate
Vice Presidents: Leo R. Armatis, Corporate Relations; Thomas G. Fisher,
General Counsel and Secretary; Larry D. Hartsook, Finance; Michael A. Sell,
Treasurer; Kathleen J. Zehr, Controller and Assistant Secretary

WE CARE!

The editors of Better Homes and Gardens Books assembled this collection
of projects and recipes to enhance your holiday enjoyment. Our staff is
committed to providing you with clear and concise instructions so that
you can create tasty foods and festive decorations and gifts. We guarantee
your satisfaction with this book for as long as you own it. We welcome
your comments and suggestions. Please address your correspondence to
Better Homes and Gardens Books, 1716 Locust Street, BB 117,
Des Moines, Iowa 50309-3023.

Our seal assures you that every recipe in Christmas at Home has been
tested in the Better Homes and Gardens® Test Kitchen. This means
 that each recipe is practical and reliable, and meets our high
standards of taste appeal.

Introduction

Each year, as the days shorten and the air
becomes crisp and cold, we prepare for the
joyful season of Christmas.

Wherever we are, it is to home our hearts travel.
Family and friends gather around the tree,
made festive with handmade ornaments.
Candles glow, children carol and the faces we love
smile as presents crafted just for them are opened.

Enjoy the holiday spirit early by crafting gifts,
baking treats and decking the halls.
This is the year to make special
Christmas memories.

Table of Contents

Decorating the Home

Gifts for Giving

Children's Crafts

A Christmas Feast

Food Gifts

Gingerbread Tree Skirt

Materials:

- One 54-inch of square red-and-green woven plaid fabric
- ³/₄ yard of light tan suede-look fabric
- 6¹/₄ yards of 1-inch-wide cotton piping
- 1 yard of 1¹/₂-inch-wide wire-edged ribbon, red with green edging
- 1¹/₄ yards of 1-inch-wide red-and-green plaid ribbon
- ¹/₃ yard of ¹/₄-inch-wide red satin ribbon
- Glossy black slick paint
- 28 inches of string
- Straight pins
- Black fabric marking pen
- Pinking or scalloping shears
- Graph paper
- Glue gun/glue sticks

Step 1

Place plaid fabric square on flat work surface. Fold square in half, right sides together. Fold in half again (see below).

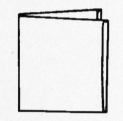

Use straight pin to attach one end of string to folded point of fabric square. Tie opposite end of string around fabric pen, leaving 25 inches of string between corner and pen. With string stretched evenly, use pen to draw a curved line from one corner to the opposite corner of fabric (see below).

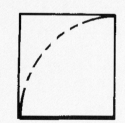

Step 2

Use pen and string again to draw a circle approximately 3 inches in diameter on center point of fabric fold. Use shears to cut large circle shape out of folded fabric. Cut out center circle before unfolding fabric. Unfold fabric. Cut a slit from outer edge to center hole (see below). Sew a 1¹/₂-inch hem around inner circle edge. Sew red piping around outer edge.

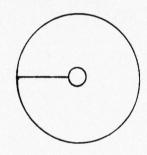

Step 3

Use graph paper and pen to enlarge gingerbread boy pattern to full size (see pattern, page 11).

Cut out pattern. Pin pattern to tan fabric. Use shears to cut out 8 gingerbread boys. Pin figures to skirt in pairs (see right). Sew figures to skirt, stitching approximately ¹/₄ inch from edge.

Step 4

Cut 1¹/₂-inch-wide red ribbon into 4 equal pieces. Make single bows (see page 154). Set bows aside. Cut four 1¹/₂-inch pieces from plaid ribbon. With hot glue, attach these pieces around centers of red bows. With hot glue, secure red bows to neckline of one gingerbread boy of each pair.

Cut remaining plaid ribbon into 4 equal pieces. Use each piece to make a single bow (see page 154). Cut narrow red ribbon into 4 equal pieces. With hot glue, attach red ribbon around centers of plaid bows. Secure plaid bows to necklines of remaining gingerbread boys.

Step 5

With slick paint make eyes, nose, mouth and buttons on gingerbread boys. Allow approximately 6 hours for paint to dry completely.

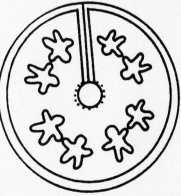

Gingerbread Pillows

Materials:

- Two 13-inch squares of red woven fabric
- Two 6½-inch squares of woven plaid fabric
- One 8½-inch square of light tan suede-look fabric
- 1½ yards of ¾-inch-wide twisted red satin cord
- 8 inches of 1½-inch-wide red-and-green plaid ribbon
- 2 inches of ½-inch-wide green plaid ribbon
- Glossy black slick paint
- Cotton batting
- Graph paper
- Fabric marker
- Straight pins
- Red thread and needle
- Iron
- Pinking or scalloping shears
- Glue gun/glue sticks

Step 1

Fold each plaid fabric square along the diagonal, from corner to corner, to form triangles (see below).

Cut along diagonal line to form 4 equal triangle shapes. For pillow top, stitch triangles, right sides together, as shown below. Press seams.

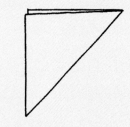

Step 2

Use graph paper and pen to enlarge gingerbread boy to full size (see pattern, page 11). Cut out pattern. Pin pattern to tan fabric. Use pinking or scalloping shears to cut out. Position figure on center of pillow top. Pin boy in place and sew to fabric, using a ⅛-inch seam allowance.

Step 3

Place second red square face down onto pillow top. Stitch around outer edges, using a ¼-inch seam allowance. Leave a 4-inch opening. Turn pillow right side out. Press seams. Stuff pillow firmly with batting. Hand-stitch opening closed.

Step 4

Attach cord around outer edge of pillow with hot glue or hand-stitch cord in place.

Step 5

Use 8-inch piece of ribbon to make single bow without streamers (see page 154). Use hot glue on center of bow to secure. Attach remaining ribbon piece around center of bow. Use hot glue to secure bow to boy's neckline for a bow tie.

Step 6

With slick paint make eyes, nose, mouth and buttons on gingerbread boys. Allow approximately 6 hours for paint to dry completely.

Small Gingerbread Pillows

Materials:

- Two 9-inch squares of red woven fabric (for one red pillow)
- Two 9-inch squares of green woven fabric (for one green pillow)

Follow instructions for Large Gingerbread pillows using green woven fabric for one pillow and red woven fabric for the other.

For one pillow:

- Two 4½-inch squares of woven plaid fabric
- One 5-inch square of light tan suede-look fabric
- 1 yard of ¾-inch-wide twisted red satin cord
- 5 inches of ½-inch-wide red-and-green plaid ribbon
- 3 inches of ⅛-inch-wide red satin ribbon
- Glossy black slick paint
- Graph paper
- Fabric marker
- Straight pins
- Coordinating thread and needle
- Pinking or scalloping shears
- Iron
- Glue gun/glue sticks

Gingerbread Dolls

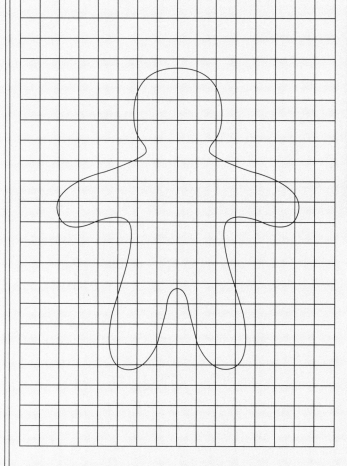

Materials:

❖ 1 yard of light tan suede-look fabric
❖ ¾ yard of 1-inch-wide green plaid ribbon
❖ ½ yard of 1½-inch-wide red plaid ribbon
❖ Glossy black slick paint
❖ Cotton batting
❖ Graph paper
❖ Fabric marker
❖ Straight pins
❖ Pinking or scalloping shears
❖ Glue gun/glue sticks

Step 1

Use pen and graph paper to enlarge doll pattern to full size (see above left). Cut out pattern. Pin pattern to tan fabric and cut out 4 doll shapes. Stitch 2 shapes, right sides together, using a ³/₈-inch seam allowance. Leave a 3-inch opening on top of doll's head. Turn right side out.

Stuff doll firmly with batting. Hand-stitch opening closed. Repeat process for second doll.

Step 2

Use green ribbon to make a large double bow (see page 155). Use hot glue to attach bow to top of one doll's head. Use red ribbon to make a large single bow. Attach this bow to neckline of remaining doll.

Step 3

With slick paint make eyes, nose, mouth and buttons on gingerbread dolls. Allow approximately 6 hours for paint to dry completely.

Gingerbread Sizes

For the small green pillow	4 ⅛ inches high x 3 ½ inches wide
For the small red pillow	4 ⅛ inches high x 3 ½ inches wide
For the large red pillow	7 ½ inches high x 6 ½ inches wide
For the tree skirt	9 ½ inches high x 8 inches wide
For the stuffed doll with tie	15 ¾ inches high x 12 ¾ inches wide
For the stuffed doll with bow	15 ¾ inches high x 12 ¾ inches wide

Cherry-Walnut Wreath

Materials:

* One 12-inch-diameter moss wreath base
* 100 to 110 artificial red, deep red and purple-red cherries
* 10 to 15 artificial green leaves
* 25 to 30 artificial holly leaves
* 20 to 25 dried holly leaves
* 35 to 40 small pinecones
* 25 to 30 rose hips
* 25 to 30 walnuts
* 5 yards of ¾-inch-wide wire-edged ribbon, teal with gold edge
* 6 inches of florist's wire
* Glue gun/glue sticks

Approximate numbers are given for decorative materials on this wreath. A very full effect is desired and exact sizes of materials will vary.

Step 1

Cut ribbon into 5 equal pieces of 1 yard each. From each yard cut one 6-inch piece. Use larger pieces to make five triple bows (see page 155). Tie one of the shorter ribbon pieces around each bow center to create extra streamers. With hot glue, attach bows to wreath, spacing evenly.

Step 2

Use hot glue to attach cherries, leaves, pinecones, rose hips and walnuts. Place materials as closely as possible to create a very full look. This wreath may be scented by adding a few drops of cherry- or Christmas-blend scented oil to mossy back.

Step 3

To form a hanger, thread wire through moss on back of wreath. Twist wire ends together to form a loop.

Christmas joy is in my heart

Cardinal Ornament

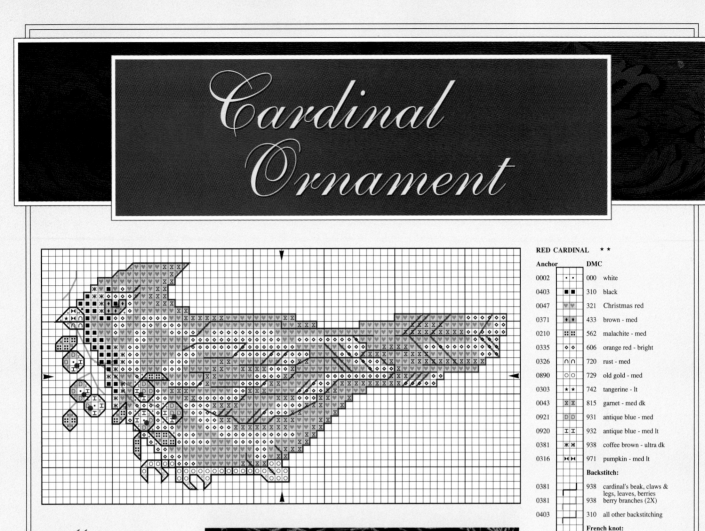

Materials:

- One 9x6-inch piece of 14-count ivory Aida cloth
- One 9x6-inch piece of lightweight fusible interfacing
- One 9x6-inch piece of ivory fabric
- Embroidery floss (see color key for colors)
- 5 inches of ⅛-inch-wide red grosgrain ribbon
- Cotton batting
- Ivory sewing thread and needle
- Clothespin (optional)

Step 1

Using 3 strands of embroidery floss for cross-stitch, center and stitch the design, above, on the Aida cloth.

Step 2

Following manufacturer's instructions, fuse interfacing to back of stitched fabric. Trim stitched fabric ¾ inch beyond design on all sides. Using stitched fabric as a pattern, cut ivory fabric to use as the backing.

Step 3

To make a hanger for ornament, fold red ribbon in half. With raw edges even, tack ends to the top of the back edge of stitched fabric, ½ inch from the back of the cardinal's head.

Step 4

With right sides together and using a ⅜-inch seam allowance, sew stitched fabric and backing piece together, leaving a 1¾-inch opening on bottom edge. Trim seams, clip curves and turn right side out.

Step 5

Fill ornament with batting. Slip-stitch the opening closed.

To make this a clip-on ornament, paint a wooden clothespin with green acrylic paint. Allow paint to dry completely and then with hot glue, attach the clothespin to the bottom edge of the ornament.

Antiqued Birdhouse

Materials

- 1 medium wooden barn birdhouse
- Red, cream and green acrylic paint
- Raw umber artist's oil or alkyd paint
- 3 or 4 sponge or synthetic fiber brushes
- 1 clean, soft rag
- Paint thinner
- Paint primer
- Wood putty
- Matte varnish
- Sandpaper

All sizes and shapes of birdhouses can be painted with this beautiful antiqued finish. Try combinations of red, green and cream for a birdhouse display this Christmas.

Step 1

Prepare the birdhouse for painting by filling in the nail holes and cracks with wood putty. Using sandpaper, smooth patches. Spray or paint house with one coat of primer. Allow primer to dry completely. Sand again.

Step 2

Using a thin coat of paint, paint the roof, door braces and door handle with green paint; the barn and chimney with cream paint; and the base, door and chimney top with red paint. Allow paint to dry completely. The primer coat will show through the base coat.

Step 3

Moisten the clean rag with paint thinner. Place a small amount of raw umber on rag. Rub into the base coat. This will darken the colors and give an antiqued effect. Add raw umber to the rag as needed. Pay special attention to the edges of the birdhouse, where "old" paint is naturally darker.

Step 4

Finish with 2 or 3 coats of matte varnish applied with a brush. Allow varnish to dry completely between each coat.

Cardinal Wreath

Materials:

- One 12-inch silver artemisia wreath base
- 5 artificial cardinals
- 18 artificial raspberries
- 21 to 24 small pinecones
- 8 to 10 small gingerbread boy buttons
- 30 to 35 dried or preserved holly leaves
- Small amount assorted greenery
- 1 yard of 1½-inch-wide red-and-green plaid ribbon
- 6 inches of florist's wire
- Pinking or scalloping shears
- Glue gun/glue sticks

Approximate numbers are given for decorative materials on this wreath. A very full effect is desired and exact sizes of materials will vary.

Step 1

With hot glue secure holly leaves and greenery to wreath base. Attach raspberries and pinecones in groups of three, distributing evenly.

Step 2

Cut one 12-inch piece of ribbon and set aside. With remaining ribbon make a double bow, 4 inches wide overall (see page 155). Secure bow center with a twist of wire. Tie 12-inch length around bow center to form streamers. Use shears to finish streamer ends in an inverted "V" shape. Secure bow to lower right-hand curve of wreath.

Step 3

With hot glue add gingerbread boy buttons to wreath, distributing evenly. Secure ornaments and cardinals to wreath, distributing evenly.

Step 4

To form hanger, thread florist's wire through back of wreath. Twist wire ends together to form a loop.

Frosted Fruit Wreath

Materials:

- ❖ One 11x12-inch heart-shaped twig wreath
- ❖ 3 small artificial deep red apples
- ❖ 4 small artificial green apples
- ❖ 12 artificial blackberries
- ❖ 18 to 20 small green, deep red and purple artificial berries
- ❖ 6 small artificial red roses
- ❖ 1 bunch preserved greenery
- ❖ 1¼ yards of 2-inch-wide red, gray and white plaid wire-edged ribbon
- ❖ 1¼ yards of 2-inch-wide green, gray and white plaid wire-edged ribbon
- ❖ 6 inches florist's wire
- ❖ 1 package hoarfrost (mica flakes)
- ❖ Spray adhesive
- ❖ Glue gun/glue sticks

Step 1

Using hot glue, attach sprigs of greenery to front of wreath form. Allow tips of greenery to feather out toward wreath center and sides.

Step 2

Using hot glue, attach fruits and berries to greenery. Distribute colors and sizes of material evenly. Secure blackberries in groups of three.

Step 3

Hold lengths of ribbon together and form a bow with two loops of each color on each side of the bow. Streamers should measure approximately 4 inches in length. Finish streamer ends in an inverted "V" shape. Secure bow to centerpoint on top of wreath.

Step 4

In a well-ventilated area, lightly spray wreath, including bow, with spray adhesive. Sprinkle hoarfrost on wreath.

Step 5

To form hanger, thread wire through twigs on centerpoint of wreath back. Twist wire ends together to form a loop.

Frosted Fruit Candle Ring

Materials:

- ❖ 1 artificial pine candle wreath base with snow
- ❖ Sphagnum moss
- ❖ 8 large artificial deep red apples
- ❖ 35 artificial holly berries
- ❖ 15 to 20 artificial green and purple berries
- ❖ 12 artificial acorns
- ❖ 20 to 25 small pinecones
- ❖ Small bunch preserved greenery
- ❖ Small bunch preserved cedar
- ❖ Artificial holly leaves
- ❖ ½ package hoarfrost (mica flakes)
- ❖ Spray adhesive
- ❖ Glue gun/glue sticks

Step 1

Using hot glue, attach moss to candle wreath base between pine stems. Cover any exposed foam or straw areas.

Step 2

Using hot glue, secure fruit, berries, pinecones and acorns to wreath base between pine stems. Attach cedar and greenery sprigs to arrangement to fill in any gaps.

Step 3

In a well-ventilated area, lightly spray candle wreath base with spray adhesive. Sprinkle hoarfrost onto arrangement. Place candle into center of candle ring.

Christmas Wreath Afghan

Materials:

- Caron Sayelle 4-ply worsted weight yarn (3.5 ounce skeins) in the following colors: 11 skeins No. 1062, Dark Sage Green, 7 skeins No. 3002, Off-white, 1 skein No. 1024, Devil Red
- Aluminum crochet hook, size H
- 8 yards of 1/2-inch-wide red ribbon, cut into 8-inch lengths for bows

Finished afghan, composed of 35 blocks, measures 51x69 inches. Each block is 9 inches square; ribbed border is 2 inches wide.

Stitches used: chain, slip stitch, single crochet, double crochet

Gauge: Over solid double crochet test swatch, 3 stitches = 1 inch; 2 rows = 1 inch

Knitting and Crocheting Abbreviations

Beg	begin(ning)
bet	between
CC	contrasting color
ch(s)	chain(s)
cont	continue
dc	double crochet
dec	decrease
grp	group
inc	increase
k	knit
LH	left-hand
lp(s)	loop(s)
lsc	long single crochet
MC	main color
p	purl
pat	pattern
psso	pass sl st over
rem	remain(ing)
rep	repeat
RH	right-hand
rnd	round
RS(F)	right side (facing)
sc	single crochet
sk	skip
sl	slip
sl st	slip stitch
sp	space
ssk	slip, slip, knit
st(s)	stitch(es)
st st	stockinette stitch
tbl	through back loop
tog	together
WS(F)	wrong side (facing)
yo	yarn over
*	repeat from *as indicated
**	repeat from ** as indicated
()	repeat between () as indicated
[]	[] — repeat between bracket as indicated

Step 1

Make 35 blocks as follows: Starting at center with Off-White yarn, ch 8, sl st to form ring.

Round 1: Ch 3, 23 dc in ring, join with sl st in top of beginning ch-3. Fasten off.

Round 2: Attach Dark Sage Green with sc in any dc. Make sc in all sts around. Join with sl st in first sc made (24 sc).

Round 3: Ch 9, sk first ch from hook, sc in rem 8 ch, sl st on ring in same place as joining, turn.

Step 2

To work main body of wreath in Dark Sage Green:

Row 1: Working in back lp only, sc in 8 sc. Ch 1, turn.

Row 2: Make sc in back lp of first 6 sc, sl st in back lp of seventh sc. Leave eighth sc unworked. Turn.

Row 3: Sc in back lp of 6 sc. Ch 1, turn.

Row 4: Sc in back lp of 6 sc. Sc over sl st, sc in back lp of eighth sc on previous long row. Sl st through next dc on ring. Turn.

Row 5: Sc in back lp of 8 sc. Ch 1, turn.

Row 6: Sc in back lp of 8 sc, sl st through next dc on ring. Turn.

Repeat Rows 1 to 6 for wreath. End with Row 5 after sl st has been made in last dc on ring.

Step 3

Fold work in half, right sides together to join. With first row of wreath on top of last row made, sl st edges together by putting hook through starting ch at bottom of first sc, and through back lp of corresponding sc on row just made. Rep in rem sc, fasten off green.

Step 4

Round 4: Attach Off-White with sl st in end of any sc row on wreath. Ch 3, make (2 dc, ch 3, 3 dc) in same place. *Ch 2, sk ends of 3 green rows. Sc in ends of next 11 rows, ch 2, sk ends of next 3 rows. Make (3 dc, ch 3, 3 dc) in end of next row. Repeat from * around. End with sl st in top of beginning ch-3.

Round 5: Sl st in next 2 dc and in ch-3 sp. Make (2 dc, ch 3, 3 dc) in same sp. *Ch 1, 3 dc in ch-2 sp. Ch 1, sk 2 sc, sc in 7 sc, ch 1, sk 2 sc, 3 dc in ch-2 sp, ch 1. Make (3 dc, ch 3, 3 dc) in corner ch-3 sp. Repeat from * around. Join in beginning ch-3.

Round 6: Sl st in next 2 dc and in ch-3 sp. Ch 3, make (2 dc, ch 3, 3 dc) in same sp. *(Ch 1, 3 dc in next ch-1 sp) twice, Ch 1, sk 2 sc, dc in next 3 sc, (ch 1, 3 dc in next ch-1 sp) twice. Ch 1, make (3 dc, ch 3, 3 dc) in corner sp. Repeat from * around. Join.

Round 7: Sl st in next 2 dc and in ch-3 sp, ch 3, make (2 dc, ch 3, 3 dc) in same sp. *(Ch 1, 3 dc in next ch-1 sp) 6 times. Ch 1, make (3 dc, ch 3, 3 dc) in corner sp. Repeat from * around. Join. Fasten off.

Round 8: Attach green by making 3 sc in any corner sp. Work sc in each dc and ch-1 sp around, with 3 sc in all corners. Join in first sc and fasten off.

Step 5

Use green yarn in tapestry needle to sew blocks together in 5 rows of 7 squares each. Experienced workers may wish to join blocks by crocheting together as Round 8 is being made.

Step 6

To make the border:

Round 1: After all blocks have been joined, attach green by making sc in any sc along side. Work sc in each sc around afghan, with 3 sc at each corner. Sl st in first sc made and fasten off green.

Round 2: Work in sc same as Round 1, using red yarn.

Step 7

Start to work wide rib section of border in rows. Attach green with sl st in any red sc along side of afghan. Ch 9, sk first ch from hook, sc in rem 8 ch, sl st in each of next 2 sc on edge of afghan. Turn.

RIB: Row 1: Working in back lp only, sc in 8 sc. Ch 1, turn.

Row 2: Sc in back lp of 8 sc, sl st in each of next 2 sc along edge of afghan. Turn.

Repeat Rows 1 and 2 along edge until only 1 or 2 sts from next corner.

Step 8

To turn corner:

Row 1: Sc in back lp of 8 sc. Ch 1, turn.

Row 2: Sc in lack lp of 6 sc, sl st in back lp of seventh sc. Turn.

Row 3: Sc in back lp of 6 sc. Ch 1 turn.

Row 4: Sc in back lp of 6 sc. Sc over sl st, sc in back lp of eighth sc of Row 1. Sl st in next sc along edge of afghan. Turn. Repeat Rows 1-4 of corner 3 times more for a total of 4 short row increases around corner sts. After last Row 4 repeat is made, sl st in next 2 sc along edge of afghan. Start again to work the previous 2-row repeat of border as before along next side. Finish other sides and corners in the same manner. End by joining edges with sl st as was done with green rib section of afghan blocks.

Step 9

To finish, tie each ribbon length into a bow. Sew as trim onto each wreath.

Mantle Garland

Materials:

- ❖ One 10-foot artificial greenery garland
- ❖ One 10-inch artificial greenery wreath
- ❖ One 7-inch brass French horn
- ❖ 12 artificial holly picks
- ❖ Six 5- or 6-inch pinecones
- ❖ 3⅓ yards of 2½-inch-wide red moiré wire-edged ribbon
- ❖ 2⅔ yards of 1¼-inch-wide red plaid ribbon
- ❖ Florist's wire
- ❖ 1 set miniature clear Christmas lights with green wire
- ❖ Scissors
- ❖ Wire cutter
- ❖ Glue gun/glue sticks

Step 1

Using florist's wire, attach wreath to center of garland. Wrap lights through garland and around wreath, keeping plug at one end.

Step 2

Cut 5 feet of red wire-edged ribbon. Make a large, 8-loop bow (see page 155 for fuller bows). Secure bow center with a twist of wire. Use 2 feet of red wire-edged ribbon to make a bow streamer. Wrap around bow center. Cut streamer ends in an inverted "V" shape.

Cut 3 feet of plaid ribbon. Make a triple bow (see page 155). Secure center with a twist of wire. Use 2 feet of plaid ribbon to make a bow streamer. Wrap around bow center. Cut streamer ends in an inverted "V" shape.

Step 3

Using florist's wire, attach plaid bow to center of red bow. Use wire to attach bows to wreath at the point where it joins garland. Use wire to add French horn just below bow. Tie plaid streamer to horn to cover wires. Arrange other streamers as desired. Secure streamers in place with hot glue.

Step 4

Cut remaining ribbon lengths in half. Attach plaid ribbon to red wire-edged ribbon with dots of hot glue every few inches. Cut ends in an inverted "V" shape. Attach to garland, distributing evenly.

Step 5

With hot glue, secure one holly pick into bow just above French horn. Attach 3 holly picks to wreath and 4 on each side of garland, distributing evenly. Use wire to secure pinecones to garland, distributing evenly.

Wooden Snowmen

Materials:

For large snowman:
- One 4x6x10-inch piece of fir for body
- One 2x2x3-inch piece of pine for hat
- ½-inch piece of ³/₁₆-inch dowel
- ½-inch piece of ¼-inch dowel
- One 6x12-inch piece of black felt
- One 1¼x22-inch strip of plaid wool

Large snowman is 10½ inches tall.

For small snowman:
- One 2x6x8-inch piece of pine for body
- One 2x2x1-inch piece of pine for hat
- ½-inch piece of ¹/₁₆-inch dowel
- ½-inch piece of ⅛-inch dowel
- One 1x14-inch strip plaid wool fabric
- One 4x7-inch piece of black felt

Small snowman is 7½ inches tall.

Materials for both:
- Shader brush
- Fine-line brush
- White, black and orange acrylic paint
- Water-based antiquing medium
- Matte varnish spray
- Four 3- or 4-pronged twigs for arms
- Graph paper
- 6 axle pins, shanks cut to ³/₁₆ inch, for buttons
- Drill
- ¼-inch, ³/₁₆-inch and ⁷/₃₂-inch drill bits
- Jigsaw or band saw
- Router or sander
- Sandpaper
- Tack cloth
- 2 yards of jute twine, cut into 1-yard pieces
- Scissors
- Craft glue

Step 1

With pencil and graph paper, enlarge snowman pattern pieces to full size (see next page). Cut out patterns. Transfer pattern for body and hat piece to wood. Transfer patterns for hat to black felt.

Step 2

Using jigsaw or band saw, cut out body and hat pieces. Slightly router the top edge of hat piece. Using scissors, cut out felt hat. Set aside.

Step 3

Using a ³/₁₆-inch drill bit, drill holes in snowman body and hat piece. Drill arm holes at the angle illustrated on pattern. Sand wood pieces and brush away sawdust.

Step 4

Using shader brush, paint snowman body with white paint. Apply 2 even coats, allowing paint to dry completely between coats. Paint axle pins with black paint. Allow paint to dry completely.

Step 5

Using sandpaper, sand one end of a ³/₁₆-inch dowel to a point for nose. Using fine-line brush, paint nose orange. Allow paint to dry completely. Apply antiquing medium to orange nose. Let stand 5 minutes and wipe off with tack cloth. Press nose into drilled hole in face to secure in place.

Using fine-line brush and black paint, make eyes and a smiling mouth. Allow paint to dry completely. Apply a coat of spray varnish to snowman. Allow varnish to dry completely.

Step 6

Cut a small piece of ¼-inch dowel and insert into wooden hat piece. Insert other end of dowel into top of snowman's head.

Glue felt circle to top of wooden hat piece on head. Slide felt hat brim circle over other felt piece. Glue together. Tie twine around hat and make a bow.

Step 7

Using scissors, fringe ends of plaid wool fabric strip. Tie wool around snowman's neck to form a scarf. Using hot glue, secure twigs into arm holes to form arms.

For Small Snowman:
Follow directions for making large snowman, adjusting drill bit sizes as necessary for drilling holes. Use hat pattern pieces indicated for small snowman (see patterns next page).

Large
snowman
wooden hat
piece

Small
snowman
hat piece

Large hat brim

Small hat circle

Large snowman

Small snowman

Large hat circle

Small hat brim

1 square=1 inch

Knitted Santa Christmas Stocking

Materials:

- Brunswick Germantown knitting worsted (3.5-ounce/220-yard skeins),
- **One skein each of:**
  Scotch Heather (No. 480)
  Natural White Heather (No. 41000)
- 12.5 grams of Scarlet (No. 421)
- 12.5 grams of Pale Peach (No. 4004)
- 12.5 grams of Dartmouth Green (No. 444)
- 4 to 5 yards of Black (No. 460)
- One 10-gram ball of white angora (use a double strand)
- One 16-inch circular needle, size 7
- 1 set double-pointed needles, size 7
- Crochet hook, size D
- 57 small orange glass beads
- 2 tiny black doll buttons for eyes
- 1 brass jingle bell
- Bobbins
- Markers
- Large-eyed needle
- Coordinated thread and sewing needle

See page 20 for the abbreviations used in this project.

Gauge: In stockinette stitch, 5 stitches and 7 rows = 1 inch.

Finished size: 19 inches long

Except for heel and toe, stocking is worked on circular needle. Santa is worked back and forth in intarsia, using bobbins for each color area. Smaller color areas, including name, are duplicate stitches after stocking is completed.

Step 1

Stocking

Using circular needle, cast on 72 stitches of scarlet yarn. Join, being careful not to twist stitches. Place marker to show beginning of rounds. Purl 1 round. Knit 1 round. Purl 1 round. Knit 1 round. Cut scarlet yarn.

Step 2

Attach Natural White Heather and knit 11 rounds. Cut natural and attach scarlet. Knit 1 round. Purl 1 round. Cut scarlet yarn.

Step 3

Attach Natural White Heather and work the 7 rows of holly pattern, working in Dartmouth Green, (see illustration 2, next page). Cut natural. Attach Scotch Heather and work even for 3 rounds. Remove marker and cut Scotch Heather.

Step 4

With Scotch Heather, cast on 1 st on left-hand needle. Knit this st and next 43 sts (44 sts total). Place marker (pm) knit 22 sts, pm, k 7, cast on 1 st.

Turn work, purl to first marker, slip marker (sm), begin Row 1 of Santa motif on 22 sts between markers, sm, purl 44 sts. Work back and forth in rows to top of Santa chart (see chart next page).

Step 5

With Scotch Heather only, bind off 1 st at beginning of next row. Work across the row to the last 2 sts, removing markers as you come to them. Turn work so the purl side is facing. With left needle bring second st over the top of the first st to bind it off.

Step 6

Turn work again so the right side is facing. Knit st on left needle, pm to mark beginning of rounds. Knit 3 rounds in Scotch Heather. Cut Scotch Heather. Attach natural and work the 7 rows of holly pattern as before (see illustration 2). Cut natural and attach Scotch Heather. Knit 4 rounds even.

Step 7

Heel

Knit next round until 18 sts left. Do not cut Scotch Heather, but using natural, knit remaining sts of round and the first 18 sts of next round onto double-pointed (dp) needle. Remove markers during knitting. Turn work. Work short rows as follows, slipping stitches as if to purl.

Row 1: Sl 1, p 35, turn.

Row 2: Sl 1, k 34, turn.

Row 3: Sl 1, p 33, turn.

Row 4: Sl 1, k 32, turn.

Step 8

Continue working heel as established, knitting or purling 1 less st per row, until there are 10 sl sts on each side of heel and 16 sts in the middle. End with sl 1, k 16, then with yarn forward (yf) sl st from left needle to right needle. Turn.

Purl row: Yf, sl 1, p 16, sl 1, turn.

Knit row: Yf, sl first st on lift needle to right needle, yarn back, k 17, yf, sl 1, turn.

Repeat purl and knit rows until all sl sts on each side are picked up. Leave all 36 sts on dp needle. Cut natural.

Step 9

Instep

Using Scotch Heather, right sides facing, knit across 18 sts, pm to mark beginning of rounds. Knit remaining 18 heel sts, then 36 sts from top of foot, then 18 sts of heel. Work 3 rounds even.

Next round (first decrease round) k 17, k 2 together, k 34, ssk, k 17. Knit 3 rounds even.

Step 10

Next round (second decrease round) knit 16, k 3 together, k 32, sl 1-k 2 togpsso, k16. Knit 3 rounds even.

Next round (third decrease round) knit 15, k 3 tog, k 30, sl 1-k 2 togpsso, k 15. Knit 3 rounds even.

Next round (fourth decrease round) knit 14, k 3 tog, k 28, sl 1-k 2 togpsso, k 14. Knit 3 rounds even.

Next round (fifth decrease round) knit 13, k 3 tog, k 26, sl 1-k 2 togpsso, k 13. Knit 3 rounds even.

Next round (sixth decrease round) knit 12, k 3 tog, k 24, sl 1-k 2 togpsso, k 12. Knit even in rounds until 5 ½ inches from heel. Cut Scotch Heather.

Step 11

Toe

With first dp needle and natural yarn, knit 12 sts. Knit 26 sts onto second dp needle and 12 sts on third dp needle. Mark beginning of round.

Round 1: With fourth dp needle, knit to last 2 sts on first dp needle, k 2 tog.

Second dp needle: K 1, ssk, knit to last 3 sts k 2 tog, k 1. Third dp needle: Ssk, knit to end.

illustration 1

illustration 2

Round 2: Knit even.

Repeat these 2 rounds until 34 sts remain. Repeat Round 1 until 18 sts remain. Place 9 sts on top of toe on one dp needle and 9 sts of bottom of toe on another dp needle. With large-eyed needle graft toe together.

Step 12

Sew beads in place for holly as shown (see photo). Sew eyes and jingle bell as shown. Duplicate stitch your name. Sew seam and weave in all ends.

Step 13

To form a hanging loop, use crochet hook and ch 25. Cut and fasten off. Attach loop to inside of stocking.

Quilted Mittens Ornament

Materials:

- One 4x10-inch piece of red fabric
- One 4x5-inch piece of fleece
- One 8-inch piece of jute twine
- Buttonhole twist thread for quilting
- Needle
- Tracing paper
- Scissors

Mittens are 2¼ inches long.

Step 1

Trace mitten pattern (see below) onto tracing paper. Cut out pattern.

Step 2

Fold red fabric in half, right sides together. Place fabric on top of fleece. Place mitten pattern on fabric and draw around it. Repeat for a second mitten, leaving ¼ inch of fabric between mittens.

Step 3

Sew on the drawn line, leaving the wrists open. Cut out mittens, leaving a ⅛-inch seam allowance. Turn mittens right side out.

open

Step 4

Insert one end of jute twine into the wrist opening of each mitten. Sew the opening closed.

Step 5

Quilt a heart in the palm of each mitten.

Reindeer Ornament

Materials:

- ❖ One 4x8-inch piece of tan fabric
- ❖ One 5x5-inch piece of red fabric
- ❖ Cotton batting
- ❖ 2 peppercorns for eyes
- ❖ 2 small twigs for antlers
- ❖ One 8-inch piece of jute twine
- ❖ Tracing paper
- ❖ Scissors
- ❖ Glue gun/glue sticks

Reindeer is approximately 4 inches long.

Step 1

Trace reindeer head and hat patterns (see below) onto tracing paper. Cut out. Set hat pattern aside.

Step 2

Fold tan fabric in half, right sides together, to form a square. Place head pattern on fabric and draw around it. Sew on the drawn line, leaving an opening as indicated (see below) for turning.

Step 3

Cut out head, leaving a scant ⅛-inch seam allowance. Turn head right side out and stuff with batting. Slip-stitch the opening closed.

Step 4

With hot glue, attach two peppercorns to face for eyes. Attach twigs to back of head for antlers, slanting them toward the ears so the hat can be glued to the top of the head.

Step 5

Fold the red fabric in half, right sides together. Place the hat pattern on the fold and draw around it. Sew on the marked line, as indicated on pattern. Cut out the hat, leaving a scant ⅛-inch seam allowance.

Step 6

Turn up bottom edge of hat. Sew a running stitch along this edge. Gather the running stitch to fit the top of the reindeer's head. Turn hat right side out. Position and secure hat in place with hot glue.

Step 7

To form a hanger, knot the two ends of the jute twine together. With hot glue, secure the knot to the back of the head behind hat.

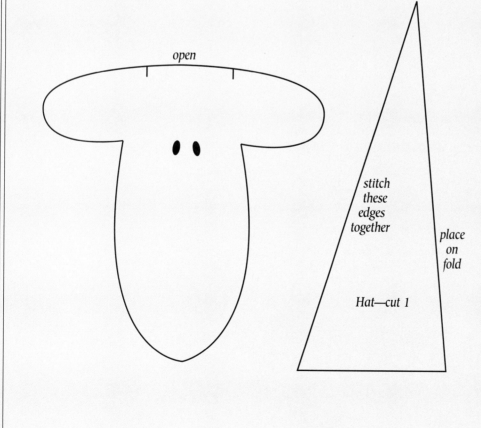

open

stitch these edges together

place on fold

Hat—cut 1

Country Santa

Materials:

- One 1½x5-inch piece of tan fabric for head
- ¼ yard of red fabric for clothing
- One 1½x16-inch piece of black fabric for legs
- One 3x8-inch piece of brown fabric for bag
- Raw wool for beard
- Cotton batting
- 15 to 20 small twigs
- Fine-line black permanent marker
- Buttonhole twist thread
- Tracing paper
- Scissors
- Glue gun/glue sticks

Santa is 12 inches high.

illustration 1

Step 1

Trace the head/body, hat and trouser patterns (illustrations 2, 3 and 4,) onto tracing paper. Cut out; set hat and trousers patterns aside.

Step 2

Cut a 3x5-inch piece from the red fabric to form the body. Match the 5-inch sides of the tan fabric for the head and the red fabric, right sides facing. Sew a seam ⅛ inch from the matched edges. Press the seam allowance toward the body.

Step 3

With right sides together, fold the stitched piece in half. Center the pattern on the fabric, aligning the dashed line separating the head from the body with the seam of the tan and red fabrics. Draw around the pattern.

Step 4

Using a short stitch length, sew on the drawn line at the top of the shoulders and the head. Stitch the side seams below the armholes, leaving the bottom open for turning.

Step 5

Cut out the head/body ⅛ inch from seam line. Clip at neckline and around curves. Turn right side out. Stuff the head only.

Step 6

To form the arms, cut a 1½x13-inch strip from the red fabric. With the right side out, fold the lengthwise edges of the strip in to the center twice. Stitch close to edge. Fold stitched piece in half and tie a knot.

Step 7

Insert raw edges into armholes and pull out at bottom of body. Stitch across raw edges (see illustration 1). Pull arms up into body. If arms are too long, pull out through bottom again, trim and stitch again. Stuff body.

Step 8

To form legs, fold the 1½x16-inch strip of black fabric in fourths. Press and stitch close to edge. Fold in half and insert into open bottom edge of body. Stitch across body, catching folded black strip in seam. Tie knots at both ends for feet (see illustration 1).

Step 9

Place right sides of red fabric together. Trace trousers pattern onto the wrong side of red fabric. Sew sides along the drawn line. Cut inner leg along the solid line (see illustration 4). Sew ⅛ inch from this cut line. Clip. Turn inside out and press.

Step 10

Fold over top of trousers ¼ inch. With buttonhole twist thread, and using running stitch, gather the waist. Put pants on Santa. Finish gathering to fit. Be sure not to position trousers too low. Tack in place with several backstitches.

Step 11

Turn under the cuff on each of the pant legs ¼ inch. Stitch with a running stitch and gather. Position trousers on leg so they billow out. Tack in place.

Step 12

Place the paper hat pattern along the fold of the red fabric and draw around it. Sew along the solid line, leaving the bottom open. Cut out hat, leaving a scant ⅛-inch seam allowance. Turn right side out.

Step 13

Turn under the bottom edge of hat. Use a running stitch and gather to fit Santa's head. Tack hat into position. If desired, hat can be bent over and tacked into place.

Step 14

With hot glue, attach a small amount of raw wool to Santa's face. With permanent marker, make 2 small dots for eyes.

Step 15

To form the bag, fold the brown fabric piece in half, right sides together. Sew up the sides, making a small curve at the bottom (see illustration 5). Turn right side out. Fold top edge of bag under ¼ inch. With buttonhole twist thread, sew a running stitch along the top to form the bag drawstring. Place small twigs inside of bag and draw top closed. Tie with a bow of thread. Stitch or glue bag to Santa's back.

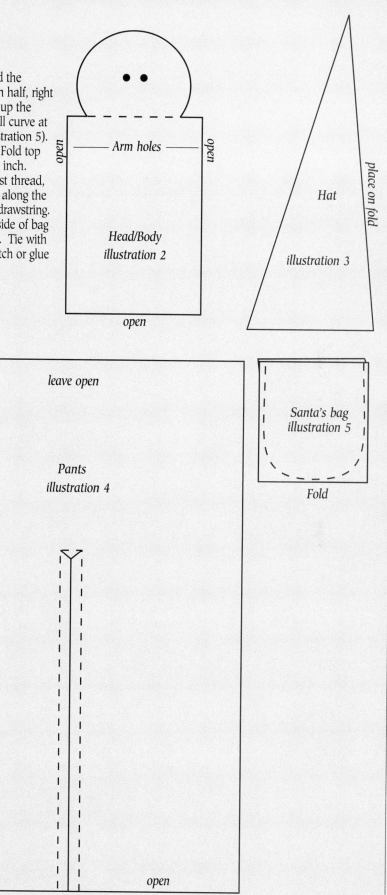

open   Arm holes   open

Head/Body
illustration 2

open

Hat
illustration 3

place on fold

leave open

Pants
illustration 4

open   open

Santa's bag
illustration 5

Fold

Courthouse Square Wall Quilt

Materials:

- ¾ yard of blue fabric for background
- ⅓ yard of red check fabric for roofs
- ¼ yard of red paisley fabric for houses
- ¼ yard of green fabric for trees
- ¼ yard of blue fabric for binding
- ⅛ yard of black fabric for chimneys
- ⅛ yard of brown fabric for tree trunks
- ⅛ yard of gold fabric for stars
- 1½-inch strips of assorted light and dark fabrics for windows and square centers
- ⅞ yard of fabric for backing
- ⅞ yard of batting
- Tracing paper
- Nonpermanent fabric marker
- Acrylic ruler
- Mat
- Rotary cutter

Wall quilt measures 26 inches square.

The pieces of this quilt may be cut using scissors and a straight edge; however, a rotary cutter simplifies the process.

Assemble the quilt into nine blocks and the blocks into three strips. The three strips are sewn together to form the quilt top.

All cutting instructions include a ¼-inch seam allowance except the star appliqué. Sew all fabrics with right sides together unless directed otherwise.

Step 1

From the green fabric cut two 4⅞-inch squares. Cut each square in half diagonally to form 4 triangles.

From the brown fabric cut one 2x22-inch strip. Press under ¼ inch along both long edges.

From blue background fabric cut two 4⅞-inch squares. Sew the wrong side of the brown strip to the right side of the blue squares as shown below.

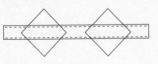

Step 2

Cut the squares apart and trim the brown fabric even with the sides of the blue square. Cut the square in half diagonally, cutting straight across the brown strip, forming 4 triangles for the tree trunks.

Step 3

Sew each tree trunk triangle to a green triangle for the tree units, as shown below. Press well.

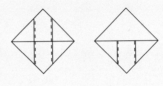

Step 4

From the blue background fabric cut four 4½-inch squares and four 4½x8½-inch strips. Sew 1 blue square to the right of 2 tree units, as shown below. Sew 1 blue square to the left of 2 tree units.

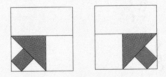

Sew on 4 ½x8 ½-inch strip to the other side of the tree unit and along one edge of the blue square.

Step 5

To make the chimneys, cut one 2⅝x22-inch strip of blue fabric. Cut one 2¾x22-inch strip of black fabric. Sew these strips together lengthwise, as shown below. Press well.

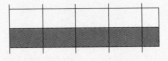

Cut four 4⅞-inch squares from the sewn strip. Cut the squares in half diagonally, as shown below. The marked triangle is used for the chimney. Discard the other.

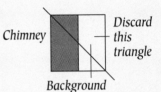

Chimney — Discard this triangle

Background

Step 6

From red check fabric cut one 9 ¼-inch square. Cut the square diagonally in both directions to make 4 triangles for the roof. Sew 1 blue triangle to the left side of each red checked roof triangle. Sew the chimney triangle to the right side of the roof triangle, as shown below. Set roof units aside.

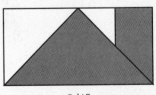

9 ¼"

Step 7

From the assorted light strips of fabric, cut sixteen 1½-inch squares. Sew 4 squares together to make 1 square window unit, as shown below. Repeat 3 times for a total of 4 windows.

Step 8

From the red paisley fabric cut eight 3½x4½-inch pieces and eight 1½x2½-inch pieces. Sew the house unit together, as shown below.

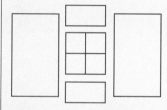

To complete the house, sew the roof design to the house unit, as shown below.

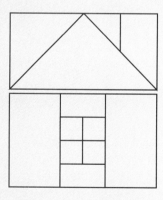

Step 9

From the blue fabric cut one 2½-inch square for the center of the courthouse steps.

From the assorted light fabrics cut two 1½x2½-inch strips, two 1½x4 ½-inch strips and two 1½x6 ½-inch strips.

From the assorted dark fabrics cut two 1½x4½-inch strips, two 1½x6 ½-inch strips and two 1½x8½-inch strips.

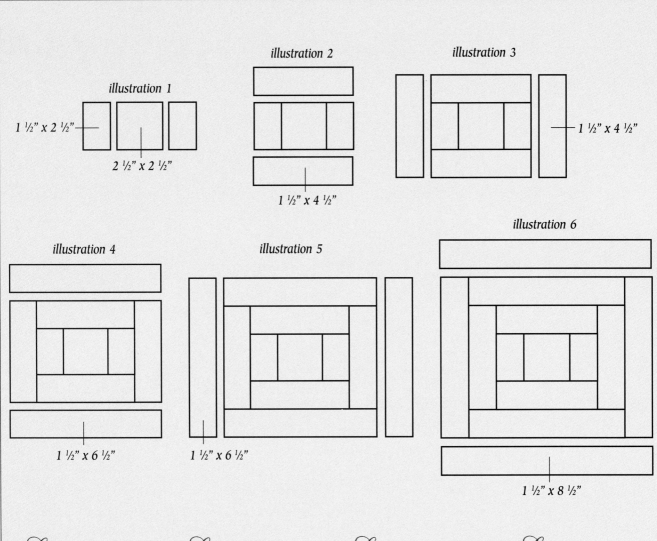

illustration 1

1 ½" x 2 ½"

2 ½" x 2 ½"

illustration 2

1 ½" x 4 ½"

illustration 3

1 ½" x 4 ½"

illustration 4

1 ½" x 6 ½"

illustration 5

1 ½" x 6 ½"

illustration 6

1 ½" x 8 ½"

Step 10

Sew the courthouse steps block, following illustrations 1 through 6, as shown above.

Step 11

Three strips form the quilt top, as shown on page 35.

To form the first strip, sew a tree design to each side of a house design. To form the center block, sew a house design onto each side of the courthouse steps. Form the third strip by sewing a tree design on each side of a house design. Press seams. Sew the three strips together.

Step 12

From the blue background fabric cut two 1½x24½-inch strips. Cut two 1½x 26½-inch strips. Sew the 24½-inch strips on opposite sides of the quilt top. Sew the 26½-inch strips to the two other sides of the quilt top.

Step 13

Using tracing paper, trace the star pattern (see below). Cut out pattern. Transfer the pattern to the gold fabric. Cut out 4 stars. Appliqué 1 star in each corner of the quilt.

Step 14

Place the batting between the quilt top and the backing fabric. Baste the layers together. Quilt as desired.

Step 15

To finish quilt, cut 115 inches of 1½-inch-wide bias or straightgrain binding strips from the blue binding fabric. Bind the edges of the quilt with the binding.

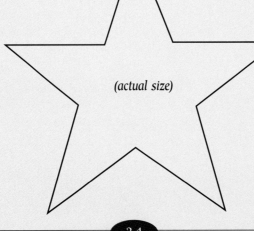

(actual size)

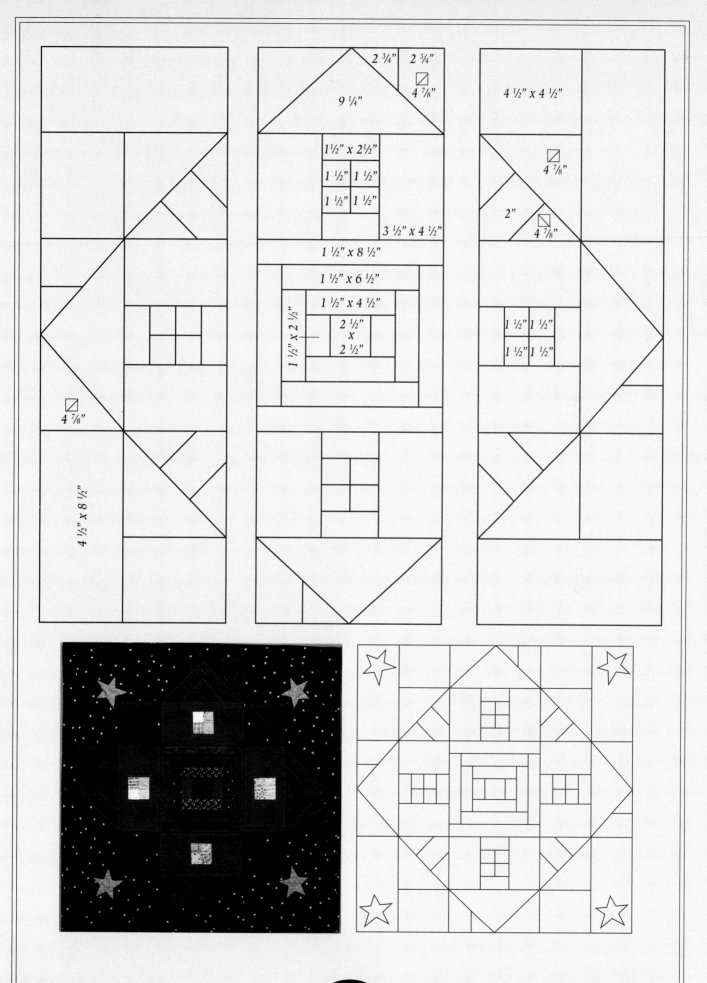

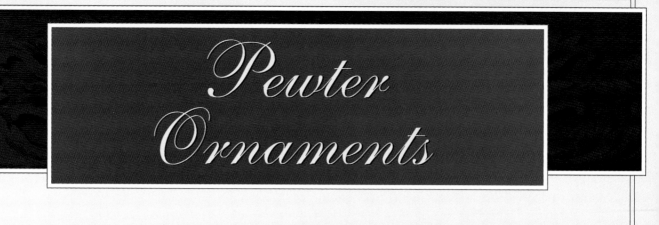

Pewter Ornaments

There are several wire-bending techniques that need to be mastered before making these ornaments. Soldering is also necessary to make one of the ornaments shown. Practice these techniques several times before making any ornaments.

Materials:

- ❖ Pewter wire
- ❖ Small wire cutter
- ❖ Needle-nose pliers
- ❖ Good quality soldering iron with small needle point
- ❖ ½ pound of 63/37 solder
- ❖ Stained glass flux
- ❖ Fine-line brush

Bending and Soldering Techniques

The Curl

Step 1

Hold wire end with pliers and bend wire until a small curl forms (see below).

Step 2

After first curl is made around pliers, wire can be bent with hands to make curl the desired size.

The Reducing Bend

Step 1

With pliers, bend a wire 2 inches from end (see below). Hold pliers on long end of wire, up against the cut end below. Bend wire in opposite direction.

Step 2

Repeat, bending wire in opposite directions, placing pliers up against the bend below. Each bend is shorter than the preceding one.

The Straight Bend

Step 1

With pliers, bend a piece of wire 1 inch from the end (see below). Hold the pliers on the long end of wire, ⅛ inch from the cut end below. Bend wire in opposite direction.

Step 2

Place pliers ⅛ inch away from first bend and bend in opposite direction. Each bend will be even with the others.

The Freestyle Bend

Bend wire with your hands, or use pliers to make curves, diamonds or squares.

Soldering

It is a good idea to practice soldering on scrap pieces of wire before making ornaments.

Step 1

Lay pieces to be joined closely together so there are no gaps between them. Dot the areas to be joined with flux.

Step 2

Hold a piece of solder in one hand and the heated soldering iron in the other. Very lightly touch the iron tip to the end of the solder. A small drop of solder will be transfered to the iron tip.

Step 3

Touch the iron tip to the wires to be joined. When it touches flux, it will sizzle and melt the two pieces together. Solder should not be visible from other side.

Step 4

To remove excess flux, wash ornaments in warm water and mild kitchen detergent.

37

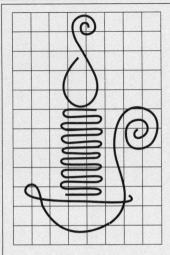

illustration 1
1 square=1 inch

illustration 2
1 square=¹/₂ inch

illustration 3
1 square=1 inch

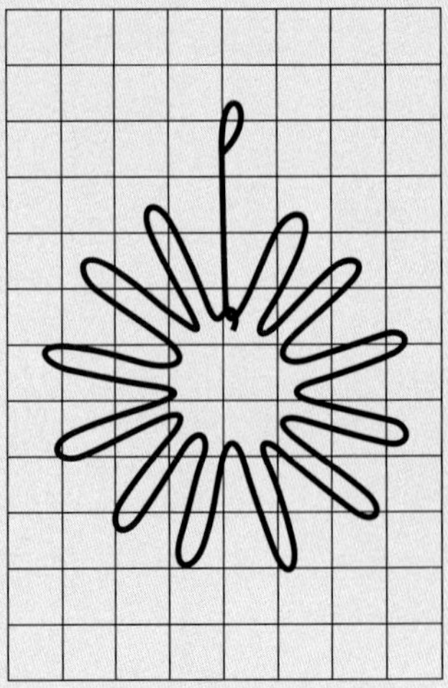

illustration 4
1 square=1 inch

The Candle

Step 1

To make the base, cut a 12½-inch piece of pewter wire. Make a curl on one end (see page 37). With hands, make curl larger to form handle. Shape rounded base with hands.

Step 2

At the left side of the base, bend wire into a small loop. Bring straight piece back around and over to meet the right side. Cut excess wire to ¼ inch. With pliers, bend the horizontal wire around right side to secure (illustraton 1).

Step 3

To make the candle, cut a 16-inch piece of wire. Make a straight bend 1 inch from the end (see page 37). Continue making straight bends until all wire is used. Remember, the height of the candle depends on the size of the bend.

Step 4

To make the flame, cut a 6-inch piece of wire. Make a curl at one end (see page 37). Bend the rest of the wire by hand to form flame (illustration 1).

Step 5

Lay all candle pieces together and solder.

The Reindeer

Step 1

Cut a 34-inch piece of pewter wire. Using the freestyle technique, begin to form the head starting with the antlers. (see above). Wire may be laid on drawing to check for size.

Step 2

Use pliers to make legs. Continue to lay the wire on the drawing to check for size and shape.

Step 3

When reindeer is formed, bend beginning end of wire around antlers to secure.

The Tree

Step 1

Cut a 30-inch piece of wire. Bend the end in 1 inch. To form the tree trunk make 3 straight bends. Form the branches by increasing the length of wire so that the next bend is 1 inch beyond the tree trunk (see above).

Step 2

Begin reducing bends until 3 inches of wire remain. Use pliers to form a curl for the tree top.

The Starburst

Step 1

Cut a 34-inch piece of wire. Make first bend ½ inch from end. Make the next bend in opposite direction, 1 inch from first bend. Work straight bends until there are 12 or 13 bends.

Step 2

Carefully bend piece into a circle, spreading bends into star shape. Cut remaining wire to 2 inches. Make a curl on top for hanger. Connect the two ends by curling the first short end around the last bottom bend.

Reindeer Table Decorations

Materials:

- 8x8-inch square of plastic foam
- 3x4-inch piece of plastic foam
- Sphagnum moss
- 1 bunch preserved cedar
- 1 bunch preserved fir
- 10 artificial silver berry stems
- 7x2-inch silver candle
- 5x2-inch silver candle
- 5 pewter reindeer (see page 38)
- 1 package hoarfrost (mica flakes)
- Scissors
- Florist's wire
- Spray adhesive
- White craft glue
- Glue gun/glue sticks

Step 1

Using wire and craft glue, center small piece of plastic foam on the large piece. Center candle next to each other on top of small piece of foam. With hot glue, secure candles to foam. Spread craft glue over all exposed plastic foam surfaces. Cover with moss. Place reindeer where desired by pushing the back hooves into foam.

Step 2

Cut greenery into 2-inch lengths. Use hot glue to attach greenery to fill gaps in arrangement. Add silver berry stems. Cover greenery with spray adhesive and dust with mica flakes.

Raspberry Candle Wreath

Materials:

- One 4¾-inch-diameter heart-shaped wreath
- Handful of red pepperberries
- 5 inches of ¼-inch-wide medium green hand-dyed rayon taffeta ribbon
- 7 artificial raspberries
- 8 to 10 lavender baby rosebuds
- 17 to 20 small, dark-colored artificial berries
- Greenery
- Glue gun/glue sticks

Step 1

Cover the wreath base with hot glue. Cover glue with pepperberries. Allow glue to set. Using hot glue, attach raspberries to wreath, distributing evenly. Secure small groupings of dark-colored berries and rosebuds to the wreath between raspberries.

Step 2

Cut greenery into small pieces and attach randomly beneath berries and rosebuds with hot glue. To form a hanger, attach the piece of ribbon to the back of the wreath using hot glue.

Raspberry and Rose Potpourri Tarts

Materials:

- 2 cups red pepperberries
- 1 cup dried miniature red rosebuds
- 1 cup mixed dried small leaves and petals
- 1 tablespoon powdered orrisroot
- 4 drops raspberry-scented oil
- 1 drop rose oil
- Greenery
- Crockery bowl
- Brown paper bag
- Clips or clothespins
- Wooden spoon

Step 1

Place orrisroot powder in bowl. Add oils and mix well with spoon. (Keep this wooden spoon separate from kitchenware after using it with scented oils.) Add botanical materials and mix well. Place potpourri in brown bag. Close securely with clips for 3 to 5 weeks to season.

Step 2

Fill 2-inch fluted tin molds with potpourri. Decorate by gluing rosebuds, cedar sprigs and an artificial raspberry to each tart.

Angel Doll

Materials:

- ⅓ yard of natural muslin for face, hands and feet
- ⅓ yard of raspberry-and-cream-striped fabric for pantaloons and sleeves
- ⅓ yard of burgundy rayon or silk fabric for skirt
- ¼ yard of floral-and-leaf-print fabric for bodice
- ⅓ yard of burgundy patterned fabric for wings
- One 18x7-inch piece of yellow knit fabric for hair
- One 18x7-inch piece of medium-weight iron-on interfacing
- ½ yard of ½-inch-wide lace trim
- 6 inches 1¼-inch-wide crocheted trim for hands
- Two 6-millimeter gold beads
- ½ yard of prestrung small gold beads for slippers
- 2 yards of prestrung medium yellow beads for hair
- 1 heart-shaped brass charm for brooch
- Burgundy carpet thread and long doll needle
- 20 inches of fishing line (optional)
- Gold acrylic paint
- Clear iridescent paint with glitter
- Round brush
- Fine-line permanent black marker
- Tracing paper
- Graph paper
- Powdered blush
- Cotton batting
- Colored pencils
- Straight pins
- Fabric glue
- Iron

Unless otherwise stated, all pattern pieces are prepared as follows: Enlarge each pattern piece to full size on graph paper. Cut out the patterns. Lay pattern on a double thickness of appropriate fabric and cut out. Stitch pieces on the line using a ¼-inch seam allowance, leaving appropriate openings. Trim seams close to stitching and turn right side out.

Step 1

Prepare body piece. To turn neck at an angle, bring neck side seams together and offset ¼ inch (illustration 3, page 44). Stitch across top of neck. Stuff toe and lower half of leg firmly. Softly stuff upper half of leg so it will bend easily. Stuff torso firmly to bottom of neck.

Lightly stuff neck. Blindstitch side opening closed.

Step 2

Prepare head. Before stuffing, lightly transfer facial features (see page 45) to front side. Stuff head firmly. Close top with gathering thread. Use pen to outline features and pupils. Color lips and irises with colored pencils. Brush cheeks with blush. Add glitter paint to cheeks and across eyelids. Pin top edge of neck to back of head approximately 1½ inches up from bottom of head. Hand-stitch neck to head. Tack underneath side of chin to neck to secure head in place.

Step 3

Using round brush, paint slippers directly onto stuffed feet with gold paint. Let paint dry completely. With glue, attach string of gold beads around edge of slippers.

Step 4

Cut out 2 pantaloon pieces. Place right sides together and stitch the inside side seams of each leg. Turn one leg right side out and slip inside other leg. Right sides of legs will be facing each other. Align all curved edges and stitch together. This forms the center front and center back seams and crotch.

Turn right side out. Turn under and stitch a narrow hem in each leg. Stitch lace trim around each leg, covering hemline. Slip pantaloons onto angel. Whipstitch top of pantaloons around waist.

Step 5

To form the bodice, cut out 2 backs and 1 front piece. Place right sides together. Stitch the backs to the front along side seams. Turn right side out and slip onto angel, opening down the back. Overlap the opening and turn under one of the raw edges. Blindstitch the opening closed.

Step 6

Cut the burgundy skirt fabric to measure 12x44 inches. Sew the short ends together. Turn under bottom edge to make a doubled ½-inch hem. Run a gathering thread around top edge. Gather to fit around waist. Secure thread and adjust gathers. Hand-stitch top of skirt waist. (Bottom of skirt should fall approximately 1 inch above bottom of pantaloons.)

Step 7

To form bodice flounce, cut 22x8-inch rectangle from bodice fabric. Fold in half lengthwise, right sides together. Stitch across ends and down long side. Leave an opening for turning. Turn right side out and press. Blindstitch opening closed. Pin ends of strip to the center of the doll's back over waist skirt. Hand-pleat strip to fit around waist. Stitch to waist. Randomly pin lower edge of flounce up in 4 different places around body. Tack in place.

Step 8

Cut a 1¾x4¼-inch strip from pantaloon fabric. Fold into thirds lengthwise. Secure around neck with glue. Overlap and turn under back edge. Secure brass charm to bodice front.

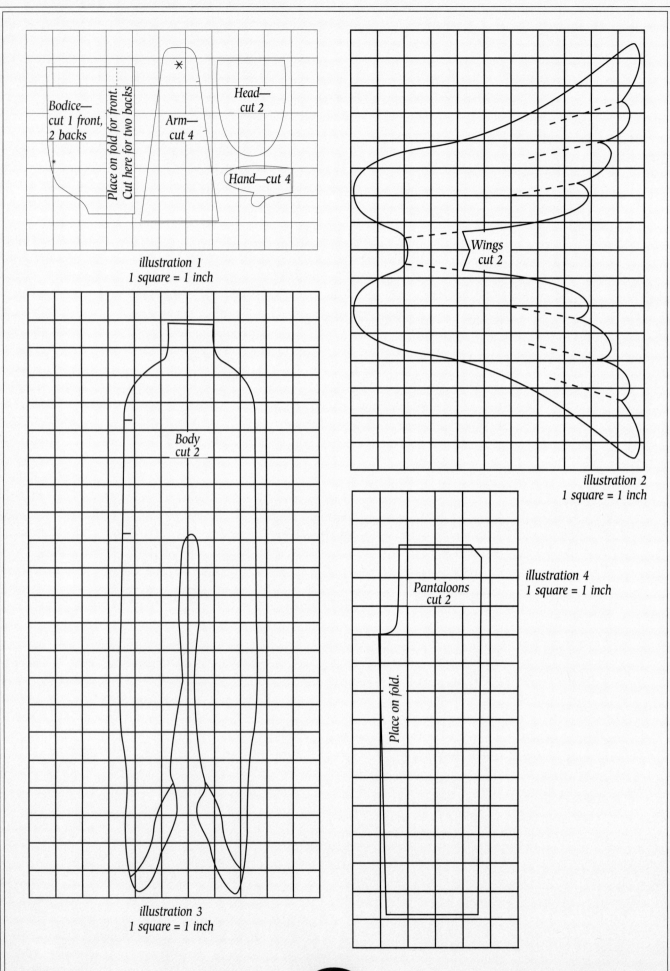

Bodice—
cut 1 front,
2 backs

Place on fold for front.
Cut here for two backs

Arm—
cut 4

Head—
cut 2

Hand—cut 4

illustration 1
1 square = 1 inch

Wings
cut 2

illustration 2
1 square = 1 inch

Body
cut 2

Pantaloons
cut 2

illustration 4
1 square = 1 inch

Place on fold.

illustration 3
1 square = 1 inch

44

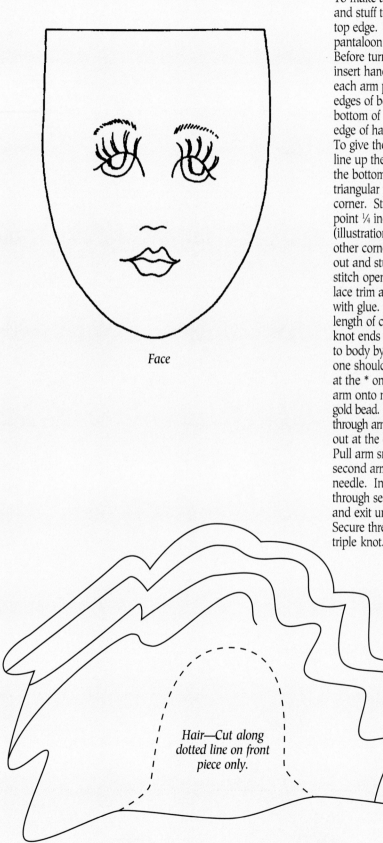

Face

Hair—Cut along dotted line on front piece only.

Step 9

To make arms, prepare hands and stuff to within ¼ inch of top edge. Set aside. Using pantaloon fabric, prepare arms. Before turning right side out, insert hands into bottom of each arm piece. Line up raw edges of both. Stitch across bottom of arm, encasing top edge of hand into seam. To give the arm/sleeve depth, line up the side seam with the bottom seam to create a triangular point at each bottom corner. Stitch across the point ¼ inch down from tip (illustration 1). Repeat for other corner. Turn right side out and stuff firmly. Blind stitch opening closed. Secure lace trim around each wrist with glue. Use a quadrupled length of carpet thread and knot ends together. Sew arms to body by inserting needle into one shoulder at the * and out at the * on opposite side. Slip arm onto needle followed by gold bead. Insert needle back through arm and shoulder and out at the opposite shoulder. Pull arm snuggly to body. Slip second arm and bead onto needle. Insert needle back through second arm and body and exit underneath first arm. Secure thread with a triple knot.

Step 10

Cut yellow knit fabric in half widthwise. Iron interfacing to wrong side of each piece. Place these pieces right sides together. Trace around outside edge of hair pattern (see below left). Stitch on line, leaving section between the dots open. Cut away excess fabric and clip corners. Turn right side out. Cut out front portion that fits around face (dotted line on pattern). Turn under bottom edge of back ¼ inch and stitch. Follow basic hair shape and glue 10 to 12 rows of yellow beads on front side of hair. When glue is dry, slip hair over head. Hand-stitch raw edge of face opening to face. Glue a row of beads around this raw edge.

Step 11

Prepare wings and stuff lightly with batting. Blind stitch opening closed. Run a row of top stitching around wings ¼ inch from edge. Following dotted lines on pattern (see illustration 2), stitch wing divisions and along fold lines. Pin wing to back of the doll above waist. Fold wings toward each other on the fold lines. Whipstitch wings to body along edges of folds.

Step 12

If you would like to hang the angel, attach one end of fishing line on top of left foot. Attach other end to angel's back, just above the top of wing. Tie a loop in the line near the top for a hanger. The length of the line and the position of the loop determine the flying position of the angel.

Holly, Mistletoe and Pinecone Ornaments

Materials

For One Ornament:

- ❖ One 6-inch square of 14-count white Aida cloth
- ❖ One 6-inch square of polyester fleece
- ❖ One 6-inch square of red pin-dot fabric
- ❖ Embroidery floss (see color key for colors)
- ❖ One 6-inch square of medium-weight cardboard
- ❖ One 6-inch square of lightweight cardboard
- ❖ 4 ½ inches of ⅛-inch-wide red grosgrain ribbon
- ❖ 4 ½ inches of ⅜-inch-wide red grosgrain ribbon
- ❖ 10 inches of ⅛-inch-diameter red twisted satin cord
- ❖ White craft glue
- ❖ Tracing paper

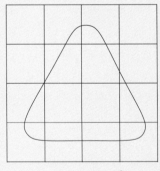

1 square = 1 inch
illustration 1

Step 1

Find the center of the Aida cloth. Using 3 strands of floss for crossstitch, stitch the design onto the Aida cloth.

Step 2

Enlarge pattern (illustration 1) onto tracing paper. Cut out pattern. Trace the paper pattern onto the back of the pin-dot fabric, fleece and both cardboard pieces. Center and trace pattern onto the back of the stitched fabric. Cut fabrics ³⁄₈ inch beyond traced line. Cut fleece and both cardboard pieces along traced line.

Step 3

Glue fleece to medium-weight cardboard. With stitched fabric right side up, center stitching on fleece. With glue, attach edges to back of cardboard. With pin-dot fabric right side up, center fabric on lightweight cardboard. With glue, attach edges to back of cardboard.

Step 4

To form a hanger, fold the ¹⁄₈-inch-wide grosgrain ribbon in half. With glue, attach ribbon ends to the top of the back.

Step 5

To create streamers, fold the ³⁄₈-inch-wide grosgrain ribbon in half at an angle. Glue fold to the center back on the bottom edge of the stitched piece. Finish streamer ends in an inverted "V" shape.

Step 6

Glue wrong sides of fabric-covered cardboard pieces together. Glue ends of twisted satin cord to prevent fraying. Beginning in the center at the top, glue the cord around the edge of the ornament.

HOLLY ★ ★

Anchor		DMC	
0020	♥ ♥	498	Christmas red - dk
0046	○ ○	666	Christmas red - bright
0258	△ △	905	parrot green - dk
0268	✕ ✕	3345	hunter green - dk
		Backstitch:	
0382		3371	everything
		French knot:	
0382	●	3371	berries

Stitch count: 27 high x 26 wide.

MISTLETOE ★ ★

Anchor		DMC	
0020	♥ ♥	498	Christmas red - dk
0301	+ +	744	yellow - lt
0258	△ △	905	parrot green - dk
0381	■ ■	938	coffee brown - ultra dk
0268	✕ ✕	3345	hunter green - dk
		Backstitch:	
0382		3371	everything

Stitch count: 24 high x 30 wide.

PINE CONES ★ ★

Anchor		DMC	
0309	⊠ ⊠	434	brown - lt
0020	♥ ♥	498	Christmas red - dk
0381	■ ■	938	coffee brown - ultra dk
		Backstitch:	
0382		3371	pine cones
0382		3371	branch (2X)
		Straight stitch:	
0258	╱	905	pine needles

Stitch count: 26 high x 31 wide.

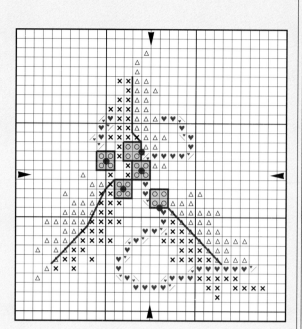

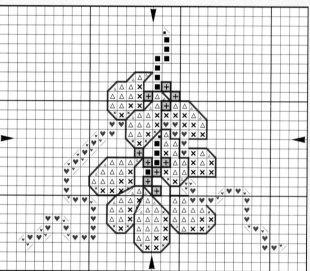

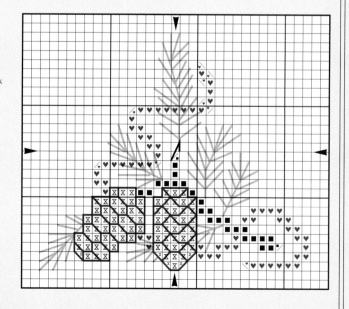

"Charlie" Snowman Ornament

Materials

For One Snowman:

- One 4x1¼-inch piece of wooden closet pole
- One ³⁄₁₆x1-inch piece of dowel
- ¼x8½-inch strip of dark wool fabric
- 3x4-inch piece of red ribbed fabric for hat
- One 6-millimeter jingle bell
- Coordinating thread and needle
- 7 inches of coordinating embroidery floss and tapestry needle
- White, black and orange acrylic paint
- Antiquing mud
- Paint thinner
- 1-inch foam brush
- Fine-line brush
- Sandpaper
- Paper towels
- Band saw
- Belt/disc sander
- Drill press
- ³⁄₁₆-inch drill bit
- Glue gun/glue sticks

Step 1

Using band saw, make 2 cuts in closet pole piece. Use sander to round and shape the cut edges. Shape the bottom end of pole. Taper one end of the ³⁄₁₆-inch dowel for the nose. Drill hole for nose (see below).

Step 2

Using fine-line brush, paint nose with orange paint. Set aside to dry. Using foam brush, paint snowman with white paint. Allow paint to dry completely before proceeding. Sand lightly.

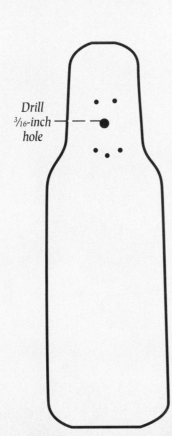

Drill ³⁄₁₆-inch hole

Step 3

Mix small amount of antiquing mud with a small amount of paint thinner until a good brushing consistency is reached. Using foam brush, apply to snowman and nose. Let stand 5 minutes. Wipe off with paper towels.

Step 4

Using the saw, cut the ³⁄₁₆-inch dowel to ½ inch. With hot glue, secure nose in place. Using fine-line brush and black paint, dot on eyes and smiling mouth. Set aside to dry completely. Spray with matte finish. Let dry completely.

Step 5

Fringe the ends of the dark wool strip. Tie around snowman's neck. Secure in place with hot glue. Fold red ribbed fabric, right sides together, so that a triangular hat is formed. Use needle and thread to stitch together. Turn right side out. Sew bell in place at top. Secure to head with hot glue.

Step 6

To form the hanger, thread embroidery floss onto tapestry needle. Take one stitch in hat and knot thread ends.

Nativity Scene

Materials:

- One 12x18-inch piece of foam-core board
- ½ yard of fusible webbing
- Six 5x6-inch pieces of assorted fabric: 3 browns for animals and manger, blue for Mary, red for Joseph and off-white for angel
- ½ yard of ⅜-inch-wide satin ribbon, colors to coordinate with clothing fabric
- 1 packet of pearl seed beads
- Gold glitter
- 6 inches of 2½-inch-wide ecru lace
- 6 inches of ¹⁄₁₆-inch-wide ribbon
- 1 tiny brass bell
- 3 off-white satin ribbon roses
- 3 inches of ⅛-inch-wide gold metallic ribbon
- 1 skein of tan embroidery floss
- Ecru sewing thread and needle
- Tan, brown, black, white, yellow and flesh-colored acrylic paints
- Fine-line brush
- Water-based varnish
- Tracing paper
- Craft knife
- Scissors
- White craft glue

Step 1

Trace all patterns, (see pages 50 and 51) onto tracing paper. Cut out patterns. Trace the patterns onto foam-core board. Using craft knife, cut out foam-core figures.

Step 2

Using the fine-line brush and acrylic paints, paint the faces and hands on all figures. Refer to photograph for ideas.

Step 3

Using the patterns, trace clothing onto the nonwebbed side of the fusible webbing. When tracing the headdresses for Mary and Joseph, trace additional length below shoulder line. Cut out.

Step 4

Following the manufacturer's instructions, fuse the webbing to the wrong side of the appropriate fabric. Cut out fabric shapes. Fuse the clothing and headdresses to appropriate foam-core figures.

Step 5

With the fine-line brush, paint the white edges of foam-core board with paints in colors similar to fabrics.

Step 6

For the cow and donkey tails, cut and combine two 10-inch lengths of tan embroidery floss. Twist the strands in a clockwise direction until the strands kink. Fold in half and let the strands twist back on each other to form a cord. Tie a knot 1½ inches from the end of the cord. Trim the raw ends to ¾ inch from the knot. Glue twisted ends of the tails to the back of each animal. Glue the knot to the body.

Step 7

Using the ⅜-inch-wide ribbon, cut and glue cuffs to the angel, Mary and Joseph. Cut and glue a front placket down the center of Mary and Joseph's clothing. Cut and glue a bottom band for the clothing on the angel, Mary and Joseph.

Step 8

Glue 3 ribbon roses to the neckline of the angel's dress. Glue the gold metallic ribbon into a circle and attach to back of angel's head. Glue pearl seed beads to the top of each ribbon cuff and the top of the ribbon band at the bottom of the angel's dress. Glue pearl seed beads down the front of the dress for buttons.

Step 9

To make wings, cut the ecru lace in half to form two 6-inch-long pieces. Sew a running stitch along one edge of lace, pull thread to gather. Tie a knot to secure gathers. Repeat for second piece of lace. Sew gathered ends together and glue to center of the angel's back.

Step 10

Spread white craft glue in the area above baby face. Sprinkle gold glitter over the glue. Allow to dry completely. Thread the bell on the 1/16-inch-wide ribbon and tie around the cow's neck. Glue ribbon to back of neck. Add a drop of glue to the back of the bell and glue to front of cow.

Step 11

To make the stands for Mary, angel and donkey, cut three 1x2¼-inch strips of foam-core board. Score one side of each strip 1¾ inch from one end. Glue the short portion of the strip to the back of the three figures, aligning the bottom of the strip with the bottom of the figures.

To make the stand for Joseph, cut a 1x3½-inch foam-core strip. Score one side 2¾ inch from one end. To make the stand for the cow, cut a 1x1¾-inch foam-core strip. Score one side 1¼ inch from end. To make the stand for baby, cut a 1x2¼-inch foam-core strip. Score one side 1¾ inch from end. Glue all stands as indicated above.

Donkey

Mary

Baby Jesus

Cow

Angel

Joseph

Holly Basket Quilted Pillow

Materials:

- ¾ yard of red fabric (A) for basket handle, triangular pieces and ruffle
- ⅓ yard of red fabric (B) for pillow back and holly berries
- ½ yard of white fabric
- ⅛ yard of green fabric (C) for triangular pieces
- Scraps of contrasting green fabric (D) for 3 holly leaves
- One 16-inch square of muslin for block backing
- One 16-inch square of quilt batting
- 2 yards of green bias piping
- One 14-inch pillow form
- Quilting thread and needle

Step 1

Cut 3½-inch-length strips from fabric A, joining with narrow seams as necessary to make a 112-inch length for ruffle. Set aside.

Step 2

Enlarge patterns to full size (see illustration 2, page 54). Make templates for pattern pieces 1 through 6.

These pattern pieces, do not include seam allowances. Using a pencil, draw around each template on the right side of the fabrics, as indicated in the materials list. Then when cutting out each piece, add a ¼-inch seam allowance.

From red fabric A, cut 1 handle (Pattern Piece 1) and 12 triangles (Pattern Piece 3).

From red fabric B, cut two 11x15-inch rectangles for pillow back and 3 holly berries (Pattern Piece 5).

From green fabric C, cut 15 triangles (Pattern Piece 3).

From green fabric D, cut 3 holly leaves (Pattern Piece 6).

From white fabric, cut 1 triangle (Pattern Piece 4), 2 rectangles (Pattern Piece 2) and a right triangle with 2 sides measuring 11 inches each and the long slant measuring 15⅝ inches.

Step 3

Piece together, stitching on pencil line, 10 of the red triangles and 10 of the green triangles to form squares. Using the red and green squares and the remaining green triangles, piece together the basket according to the illustration (see below).

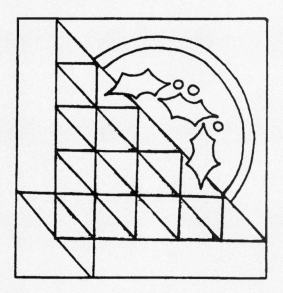

illustration 1

Following the same illustration, add one of the red triangles to each of the white rectangles. Then add one of these strips to the sides of the basket. Press seams. Then add the white triangle to the bottom corner of the basket block. To complete the pillow top, add the large white right triangle to the top of the basket. Press seams.

Step 4

To applique´ the pieced block, turn under the ¼-inch seam allowance on holly leaves, holly berries and basket handle. Arrange on basket block and appliqué in place (see below). Press the block.

Step 5

To quilt the block, place the batting between the block top and the muslin backing. Baste or pin all layers securely together. Omitting the holly berries, quilt around the inside perimeter of each piece. Quilt around the outside edge of basket handle, holly berries and holly leaves. Quilt a centerline across the holly leaves to simulate leaf markings.

Step 6

To attach the bias piping, pin the raw edges of the binding and the block together on the right side of the entire pillow block. Baste in place.

Step 7

To attach the ruffle, fold the 3½x112-inch fabric strip in half lengthwise, right side out. This forms a strip 1¾x112. Stitch two ends together to form a circle. Baste the raw edges of the strip together. Pull basting thread to gather ruffle, adjusting size to approximately a 56-inch ruffled circle.

Step 8

Pin raw edge of ruffle to raw edges on right side of quilt block. Stitch ruffle to quilt block, using same seam line as the basted bias piping (see below).

Step 9

To prepare the pillow back, turn under a ½-inch hem on one long side of each 11x15-inch red fabric B. Press hem. Fold under ¼-inch raw edge of hem and stitch (see below).

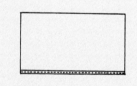

Step 10

To assemble block, pin pillow back pieces to quilt block, right sides together. The hemmed edges of the pillow back should be toward the center and will overlap approximately 5 inches (dotted line A, below, shows overlap). Align raw edges of overlapping pillow back pieces and stitch. Turn right side out and insert a 14-inch pillow form.

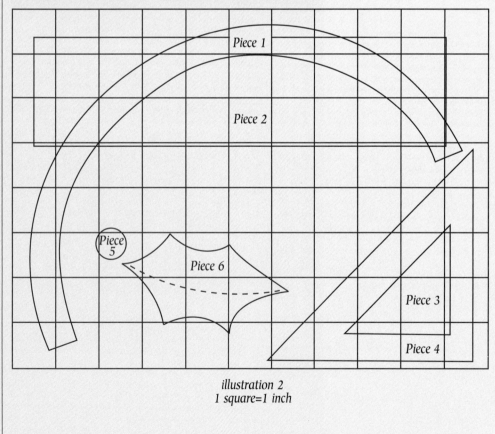

Piece 1

Piece 2

Piece 5

Piece 6

Piece 3

Piece 4

illustration 2
1 square=1 inch

Star Stocking

Materials:

- ½ yard of navy blue narrow-wale corduroy fabric
- ¼ yard of white wide-wale corduroy fabric
- ⅔ yard of ¼-inch white cord
- Nineteen ½-inch pronged gold stars
- Two 1¼-inch solid brass star charms
- One 1½-inch open brass star charm
- Two 1-inch open brass star charms
- 1⅔ yards narrow gold cord
- Navy blue and white thread and needle
- Straight pins
- Tracing paper
- Scissors
- Glue gun/glue sticks

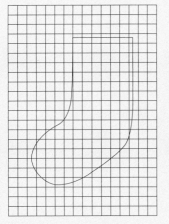

1 square=1 inch

Step 1

Enlarge pattern and trace pattern on tracing paper (see below left). Cut out patterns. Fold navy fabric in half lengthwise, nap inside. Pin pattern to fabric. Cut out. Stitch pieces together, naps inside, using a ¼-inch seam allowance. Leave top open.

Step 2

Measure 18½ inches of white corduroy and cut off. Fold in half lengthwise, nap inside. Stitch short ends together using a ¼-inch seam allowance. Turn down halfway, so that nap is both inside and outside.

Step 3

Turn navy sock right side out. Fit white corduroy just inside sock, raw edges up. Pin blue and white raw edges together. Stitch all the way around, using a ¼-inch seam allowance. Turn the white section out and down over the blue sock.

Step 4

Hand-stitch white cord to lower edge of white cuff. Trim excess. Cut an 8-inch piece of white cord. Sew a loop to the inside upper right of sock.

Step 5

Decorate sock with stars, distributing evenly. Push prongs through to wrong side of fabric and flatten with finger or pencil.

Step 6

Cut gold cord into five 12-inch pieces. Tie a star charm to the end of each piece. Gather cords together with charms at different lengths. Tie all cords into a knot. Tie bunched cords to sock loop.

Alphabet Block Wreath

Materials:

- ❖ One 12x12-inch piece of heavy cardboard
- ❖ One 12-inch piece of 24-gauge wire
- ❖ 3 yards of 5-inch-wide red paper ribbon
- ❖ Assorted large and small wooden alphabet blocks
- ❖ 10 or 12 small toys or ornaments
- ❖ Awl or nail
- ❖ Scissors or craft knife
- ❖ Glue gun/glue sticks

Step 1

Cut a 12-inch-diameter circle from the heavy cardboard. Cut a 7-inch-diameter circle in the center of the 12-inch cardboard circle.

Step 2

With the awl or nail, punch 2 holes 2 inches below the outside edge of the circle, 6 inches apart. Punch 2 more holes ½ inch from the first two holes. To make a hanger, thread the ends of the wire in one hole on each side and out the hole ½ inch away. Twist the wire ends around the longer piece of wire to secure the loop. Secure the twisted part of wire to the base with a generous amount of hot glue.

Step 3

Wrap the base with the red paper ribbon. Secure in place with liberal amounts of hot glue. This is the base to which the blocks will be attached.

Step 4

Using hot glue, attach blocks to the front of the paper ribbon-covered base. Glue a second layer of blocks on the base. Rotate the wreath so that the hanger is facing away from you before gluing a third layer of blocks to the wreath. The third layer of blocks needs to be level to provide seats for the toys or ornaments to be glued later.

Step 5

Attach toys or ornaments to blocks randomly, securing in place with hot glue. Make sure they will be upright when the wreath is hung.

Christmas Paper Wreath

Materials:

- One 6-inch-diameter twig wreath
- 1⅛ yards of ⅞-inch-wide red-and-green Christmas plaid ribbon, cut into 5-inch pieces
- 2⅛ yards of 1½-inch-wide red-and-green Christmas tartan ribbon, cut into 5-inch pieces
- 4 yards of light brown paper twist ribbon, cut into 4-inch pieces
- 15 artificial red berries
- 1 yard of florist's wire
- Glue gun/glue sticks

Step 1

Using ribbon pieces, make single bows, approximately 2½ inches wide overall, with no streamers (see page 154). Fasten bows with twist of wire. Set bows aside.

Step 2

Open the paper ribbon pieces and twist each piece in the middle to form an open bow. Using hot glue, secure twists close together on wreath.

Step 3

Secure bows to inside of twists, alternating the two ribbons.

Step 4

Glue berries in groups of three to paper twists.

"Geese are Getting Fat" Card Holder

Materials:

- ❖ One 14x12-inch piece of 14-count oatmeal Rustico Aida cloth
- ❖ Embroidery floss (see color key for colors)
- ❖ ¾ yard of green quilted fabric
- ❖ ¼ yard of red pin-dot fabric
- ❖ ⅜ yard of green fabric
- ❖ ½ yard of 2⅛-inch-wide red grosgrain ribbon
- ❖ 1¾ yards of 1-inch-wide red grosgrain ribbon
- ❖ ¾ yard of ¼-inch-wide red grosgrain ribbon
- ❖ ½ yard of ⅛-inch-wide red grosgrain ribbon
- ❖ One 22½-inch red dowel with finials
- ❖ Red and green sewing thread and needle
- ❖ Scissors

Use a ½-inch seam allowance unless otherwise noted. Sew all seams with right sides together.

Step 1

Find the center of the Aida cloth. Using 3 strands of embroidery floss for cross-stitch, stitch the geese chart (see illustraton 1) centered onto the Aida cloth. Trim fabric ¼ inch on all sides beyond design.

Step 2

Cut fabrics according to chart (see illustration 2). Using a ¼-inch seam allowance, sew strips A and B to stitched fabric in alphabetical order. Press strips away from design as you sew.

Step 3

Sew fabrics C-E to stitched fabric in alphabetical order. Press strips away from design as you sew. Sew strips F and G together along one long edge. With wrong sides together and press.

Step 4

With quilted fabric right side up, pin remaining raw edges of strips F and G to bottom and lower side edges of stitched fabric to form pocket. With wrong sides together, pin stitched fabric. Baste along all sides.

Step 5

Cut three 5½-inch pieces from the 2⅛-inch-wide ribbon. Fold each piece in half to form a loop. Baste the raw edges of one loop to the top center of the back edge of the stitched fabric. Baste the remaining two loops 1 inch from each side edge.

Step 6

Press one long edge of strips H and I under ½ inch. Sew the H strip to top and bottom of stitched fabric. Press strips away from design. Fold remaining long edges of strips to the back of the stitched fabric. Slipstitch pressed edges to back.

Step 7

Center I strips top to bottom. Sew strips to sides of stitched fabric. Fold remaining long edges of strips to back of stitched fabric and the slip-stitched pressed edges to the back. Insert dowel through loops.

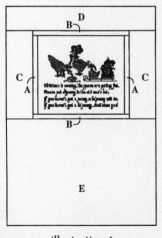

illustration 1

THE GEESE ARE GETTING FAT ★ ★

Anchor			DMC	
0002	·	·	000	white
0896	C	C	315	antique mauve - dk
0895	X	X	316	antique mauve - med
0047	□	□	321	Christmas red
0145	×	×	334	baby blue - med dk
0351	❖	❖	400	mahogany - dk
0347	∩	∩	402	mahogany - lt
0400	#	#	414	steel gray - med
0398	◇	◇	415	pearl gray - lt
0363	@	@	436	tan
0020	♥	♥	498	Christmas red - dk
0239	I	I	702	kelly green
0326	★	★	720	rust - med
0323	△	△	722	rust - lt
0306	Y	Y	725	topaz - med
0778	J	J	754	peach flesh - lt
0968	+	+	778	antique mauve - lt
0307	✳	✳	783	Christmas gold
0044	▦	▦	814	garnet - dk
0379	○	○	840	beige brown - med
0246	▲	▲	986	forest green - vy dk
0382	■	■	3371	black brown
	◄	◄	3781	mocha brown - dk
0831	◇	◇	3782	mocha brown - med lt
			Backstitch:	
0145			334	blue–checked scarf's fringe
0044			814	saying, baby goose's scarf fringe
0382			3371	everything else
			French knot:	
0382	●		3371	eyes, bear's nose, doll's buttons
0002			000	eyes of 2 geese

Stitch count: 118 high x 142 wide.

Qty.	Piece	Size	Fabric
2	A	1"x11"	red pin-dot
2	B	1"x12¾"	red pin-dot
2	C	3⅛"x11"	green quilted
1	D	3⅛"x17"	green quilted
1	E	11¼"x17"	green quilted
1	F	9"x17"	green quilted
1	G	9"x17"	green
2	H	2⅛"x17"	red pin-dot
2	I	2⅛"x 24"	red pin-dot
1	back	17"x23⅜"	green quilted

illustration 2

Christmas is coming, the geese are getting fat,

Please put a penny in the old man's hat;

If you haven't got a penny, a ha'penny will do,

If you haven't got a ha'penny...God bless you!

Christmas is coming, the geese are getting fat,
Please put a penny in the old man's hat;
If you haven't got a penny, a ha'penny will do,
If you haven't got a ha'penny...God bless you!

Materials:

- One 5-inch Spanish moss wreath
- 18 to 20 dried rose hips
- 6 whole nutmegs
- ½ cup whole cloves
- 5 to 6 artificial brown berries
- 10 small artificial red and white mushrooms
- 12 to 16 small sprigs preserved boxwood
- 1 ¾ yards of ⅜-inch-wide red cotton cord with Christmas print
- Glue gun/glue sticks

Step 1

Cut one 20-inch piece of cord. Make a single bow, 3 inches wide overall, with 3 ½-inch streamers (see page 154). Center bow and glue streamer ends to back of wreath.

Step 2

With hot glue secure one end of remaining cord to back of wreath. Wrap cord around wreath in a spiral fashion. Trim excess and secure in place.

Step 3

With hot glue secure 6 groups of boxwood to wreath.

With hot glue attach 1 nutmeg to each cluster. Attach remaining materials to groups, distributing colors evenly.

Christmas Arrangement

Materials:

- One 5x8 ½x 4-inch natural oval basket
- Florist's foam, cut to fit basket
- 1 bunch red pepperberries
- 1 bunch wheat
- Small bunch silver artemisia
- 1 bunch sweet annie
- Small bunch preserved cedar
- 1 bunch dried cupid's dart pods
- 6 to 8 pinecones
- 1 yard of 1-inch-wide garnet red grosgrain wire-edged ribbon
- Sphagnum moss
- Glue gun/glue sticks

Step 1

Place foam in basket. Cover with moss.

Step 2

Press stems of sweet annie, pepperberries and cedar into foam. Distribute materials evenly. Add remaining botanicals. Glue pinecones into arrangement to fill gaps.

Step 3

Use ribbon to make a triple bow with streamers (see page 155). With hot glue secure bow to upper rim of basket.

Oval Christmas Platter

Materials:

- One 9x14-inch oval clear glass platter
- Santa-print gift wrap
- Deep forest green and burgundy acrylic paint
- Gloss medium
- Flat brush
- Small round brush
- White vinegar
- Sponge
- Paper towel or rag
- Scissors

Step 1

Clean platter with vinegar and sponge. Rinse with water and towel dry.

Step 2

Cut out Santa motifs from gift wrap. Apply gloss medium to back of each Santa. Turn over and apply to front of each Santa. Position Santas on bottom of platter right sides up. Smooth in place to eliminate air bubbles. Allow to dry. Wipe off any excess with rag or paper towel.

Step 3

Apply an even coat of dark green paint on the back of the platter. Allow paint to dry completely. Apply a second coat of green paint and allow to dry completely. Hold plate up to light. Patch any spots where light filters through.

Step 4

Using small round brush, apply burgundy paint around edge of platter as trim. Allow paint to dry completely. Finish platter with an even coat of gloss medium. Allow to dry completely.

This platter is for decorative purposes only.

Poinsettia Topiary

Materials:

- One 6-inch clay pot
- 1 block plastic foam, cut to fit pot
- One 6-inch-diameter plastic foam ball
- Sphagnum moss
- One 14x½-inch-diameter branch
- 1 bunch preserved fir
- 1 bunch preserved cedar
- 1 bunch preserved boxwood
- 2 branches miniature variegated artificial holly
- Twelve 3-inch artificial poinsettia heads
- 3 ⅓ yards of ½-inch-wide red satin ribbon
- 1 bunch dried baby's breath
- Scissors
- Wire cutter
- White craft glue
- Glue gun/glue sticks

Step 1

Use hot glue to secure plastic foam into pot. Push branch approximately 4 inches into plastic foam block. Remove branch, fill hole with hot glue. Reinsert branch and secure with more hot glue. Push plastic foam ball approximately 2 inches onto branch. Remove ball, fill bottom of hole with hot glue and replace on branch. Spread white craft glue over entire surface of ball. Cover with moss.

Step 2

Cut all preserved greenery into 2-inch pieces. Secure to moss with hot glue and by poking into ball. Secure poinsettia heads over surface of wreath, approximately 2 inches apart.

Cut apart holly berries and baby's breath. Distribute materials evenly, securing in place with hot glue.

Step 3

Cut ribbon into six 20-inch pieces. Make a small single bow at one end of each piece of ribbon. (see page 154). Secure the bow to the base of the topiary ball where it meets the branch, allowing the streamers to hang down loosely.

Poinsettia Tea Cozy

Materials:

- One 18x24-inch piece of 18-count white Heartsong cloth
- 3 skeins of Christmas red embroidery floss
- 2 skeins each of very dark Christmas green and medium garnet embroidery floss
- 1 skein each of medium dark Christmas green, light yellow and medium dark salmon embroidery floss
- ¾ yard of red pin-dot fabric
- ½ yard of white fabric
- ½ yard of heavy polyester batting
- ¾ yard of ³⁄₁₆-inch-diameter cotton cord
- Red, white and light blue sewing thread and needle

Use a ½-inch seam allowance unless otherwise noted.

Step 1

Cut Heartsong in half to make two 18x12-inch rectangles.

Find the center of Heartsong cloth. Using 6 strands of floss for cross-stitch, stitch poinsettia and lattice chart centered over 2 threads on Heartsong.

Step 2

Using light blue thread, sew running stitches around curved edge of design (see illustration, next page). Cut stitched fabric ½ inch beyond running stitches on curved edge. Cut stitched fabric 1 inch beyond design at bottom (straight edge).

Step 3

Using stitched fabric as a pattern, cut one from remaining Heartsong (for backing), 2 pieces of white fabric (for lining) and 2 pieces of batting.

Using white thread, baste the batting pieces to the wrong sides of the stitched and backing Heartsong pieces.

Step 4

Cut and piece a 2x27-inch bias strip from the red pin-dot fabric. Using fabric and cotton cord, make piping. Trim piping seam allowance to ½ inch.

Step 5

Cut a 1¼x3-inch strip from remaining Heartsong. Fold strip in half, right sides together. Using a ¼-inch seam allowance, stitch long edges together. Turn fabric right side out.

Topstitch ⅛ inch from long seamed edge. Form a loop by folding strip in half, edges even. Baste ends to center of the top curved edge of stitched fabric.

Step 6

With raw edges even, baste piping around curved edge of stitched fabric.

With right sides together, sew stitched fabric and backing pieces together along curved edges. Trim seam and turn right side out. Repeat with lining pieces, leaving a 4-inch opening. Do not turn lining pieces.

Step 7

Cut and piece pin-dot fabric to make a 2½x62-inch strip. Sew short edges of strip together to form a loop. With wrong sides together, fold loop in half lengthwise. Press. Beginning ¼ inch from raw edges, sew 2 rows of gathering stitches around loop. Gather loop to approximately 31 inches.

With raw edges even, baste ruffle around bottom edge of stitched fabric piece, adjusting gathers as necessary.

Step 8

With right sides together, insert stitched fabric and backing into lining. Sew together around bottom edge. Trim seam and turn. Slip-stitch opening in lining. Tack lining to stitched piece at top inside edge of tea cozy.

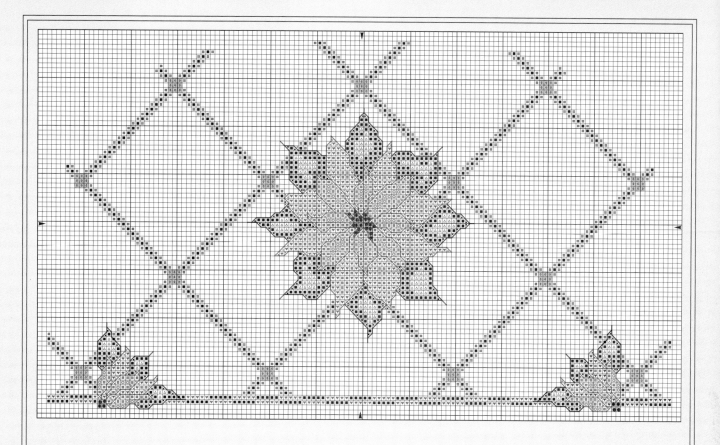

POINSETTIA ★ ★			
Anchor		DMC	
0047	# #	321	Christmas red
0923	■ ■	699	Christmas green - vy dk
0227	△ △	701	Christmas green - med dk
0301	◊ ◊	744	yellow - lt
0044	♥ ♥	816	garnet - med
0011	○ ○	3328	salmon - med dk
Backstitch:			
0923		699	leaves [2X]
0072		902	flowers [2X]
French knot:			
0297	●	743	centers of flowers (fill area) [2X]

Stitch count: 77 high x 135 wide.

Poinsettia Coasters

Materials

For one coaster:
❖ One 6-inch square of 18-count white Heartsong cloth
❖ Embroidery floss (see color key for colors)
❖ ⅛ yard of red pin-dot fabric
❖ Red sewing thread and needle

Use a ⅜-inch seam allowance.

Step 1

Measure 1 ¾ inches down and in from one corner of Heartsong cloth to find starting point. Using 2 strands of floss for cross-stitch, stitch corner poinsettia motif over thread in one corner of Heartsong. Trim 1 inch from all sides fabric. Zigzag-stitch edges.

Step 2

Cut two 1 ½x4-inch strips from pin-dot fabric (A). Cut two 1 ½x4 ¾-inch strips from pin-dot fabric (B). Turn one long edge of each strip under ⅜ inch and press.

Step 3

With right sides together, sew the long, unpressed edges of the A strips to the opposite sides of stitched fabric. Press strips away from stitched design. Fold the remaining long edge of each strip to the back of the stitched fabric. Slip-stitch pressed edges in place.

Step 4

With right sides together and B strips centered side to side, sew the long, unpressed edges to the remaining sides of stitched fabric. Press strips away from design. Press ends of strips to back of stitched fabric.

Fold remaining long edge of strips to back of the stitched fabric. Slipstitch pressed edge in place.

Herbal Christmas Wreath

Materials:

- One 15-inch straw wreath base
- 18 to 20 large pinecones
- 20 to 25 small pinecones
- 16 to 20 dried nigella pods
- 1 bunch dried flax or filler grass
- 1 bunch dried sea oats or other grain
- 1 bunch dyed red flower spikes
- 1 bunch dyed green weeping eucalyptus
- 1 bunch sweet annie
- 1¾ yards of a 6-inch-wide strip of hunter-green-striped fabric
- Two 5-inch pieces florist's wire
- Scissors
- Iron
- Glue gun/glue sticks

Step 1

Cut fabric into one 16-inch piece, one 41-inch piece and one 6-inch piece. Use 16-inch piece to make bow streamers. Fold sides inward to create a back seam, centering floral stripe on front. Press well. Using hot glue secure back seam. Finish streamer ends in an inverted "V" shape.

Twist a piece of florist's wire around center to gather. Twist wire ends together and push into straw wreath. Fold remaining pieces in the same manner, iron in place and secure back seams. Use 41-inch piece to form a double bow, with front loops 1 inch smaller than back loops (see page 155). Use hot glue to secure center folds. Use remaining piece to wrap around center of bow. Secure in place with hot glue. Secure bow on top of center of streamers.

Step 2

Using hot glue, attach pinecones and pods to wreath front, distributing evenly. Tuck small cones under bow loops. Glue green leaves, red flowers, sweet annie and weeping eucalyptus around outer edge of cone area.

Attach flax or filler grass around flowers and leaves. Attach sea oats or grain around outer edge of wreath.

Step 3

To form a hanger, use remaining wire and push one end of wire behind bow area. Twist wire ends together to form a loop.

Folk Art Santa

Materials:

- ⅓ yard of natural artist's canvas
- Barn red, brown and blue acrylic paint
- ¼ yard of deep green printed cotton fabric
- One 3x5-inch piece of plaid cotton fabric
- 1¾x7-inch piece of plaid cotton fabric
- 8x8-inch piece of fusing material
- Scraps of 4 or 5 Christmas-print fabrics
- 2 printed muslin spice bags
- 6 inches of ¼-inch-wide red satin ribbon
- 1 sprig red pepperberries
- 1 sprig preserved greenery
- One 8-inch spray sweet annie
- Selection of miniature toys
- Wavy white wool doll hair
- 2 brass bells
- Cotton batting
- Fine-line brush
- Graph paper
- Pen
- Scissors
- Newspaper
- Straight pins
- Bowl
- Sponge
- Twig wreath
- Glue gun/glue sticks

Step 1

Use graph paper and pencil to enlarge pattern pieces for Santa body and arms to full size (see page 74). Pin pattern pieces to folded canvas and cut 2 body pieces. If canvas too difficult to cut doubled, cut one section at a time.

Cut out 2 arm pieces (see pattern, page 74). Cut out 1 body piece and 1 bottom oval (see pattern, page 74). Cut out 1 large red print pocket (see pattern, page 74). Cut out 1 smaller deep green pocket (see pattern, page 74). Cut out 3 patches of mixed prints (see pattern, page 74).

Step 2

Place body pieces together. Sew together from the bottom of one side to the opposite side, using a ¼-inch seam allowance. Leave bottom open. Set aside. Fold each arm piece in half lengthwise and sew together, using a ¼-inch seam allowance. Leave bottom of arms open.

Step 3

Place 1 cup water in bowl. Add 1 to 2 tablespoons of red paint to water. Mix well to create a color wash. Place a pad of newspapers on work surface. Dip sponge in color wash and apply to Santa body and arms. Do not apply color above neckline. Paint will soak into canvas to create a soft, worn look. Allow canvas to dry completely.

Step 4

Use fine-line brush to apply red circle cheeks to Santa's face. Paint eyebrows, nose and eye outlines with brown paint. Paint eyes blue (see illustration, page 74). Allow paint to dry completely.

Step 5

Stuff body, head and arms with batting. Use hot glue to close openings. Pinch canvas to gather. Using hot glue, secure arms to body at shoulders. Attach bottom piece to Santa.

Step 6

Using the doll hair and hot glue, secure a 5-inch-long beard to Santa's face below nose. Attach a 3-inch-wide mustache on top line of beard.

Attach hair to Santa's head to form a halo around face. Secure red pocket to Santa's right side, just below beard. Overlap green pocket onto red pocket. Secure in place with hot glue.

Step 7

Using larger plaid fabric piece, make a toy sack. Fold fabric in half lengthwise. Using hot glue, secure sides together, leaving top open. Fray opening slightly. Fold top edge down ¼ inch. Following manufacturer's instructions, fuse 3 scrap patches to front of toy sack. Stuff sack with batting. With hot glue, secure toys into sack and attach sack to Santa's right shoulder.

Step 8

Use plaid fabric to make a bow. Using hot glue, attach bow to twig wreath. Attach wreath to Santa's left sleeve. Tie brass bells to red ribbon. Attach one end of ribbon to Santa's right sleeve. Secure spice sacks and a sprig of greenery to Santa's right sleeve. Fill Santa's pockets with greenery, pepperberries and small toys. Secure a crown of pepperberries and sweet annie around Santa's head.

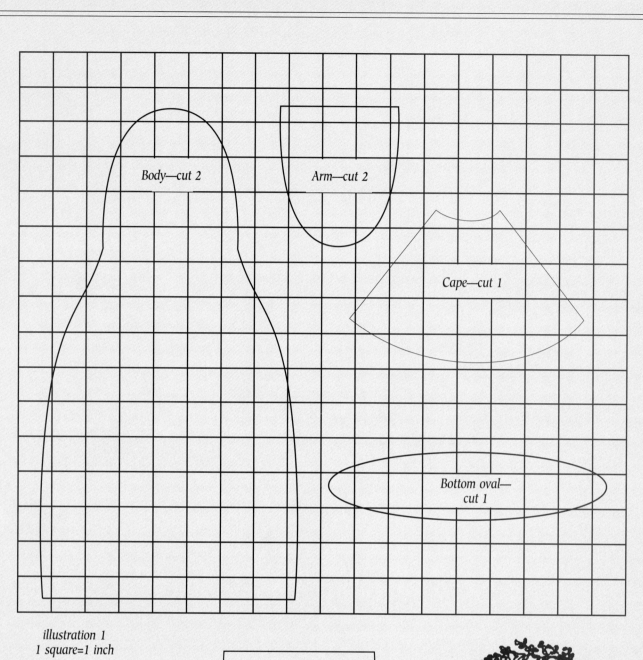

Body—cut 2

Arm—cut 2

Cape—cut 1

Bottom oval—
cut 1

illustration 1
1 square=1 inch

Pocket

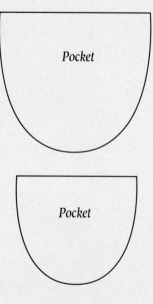

Pocket

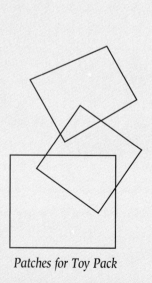

Patches for Toy Pack

Gifts
for Giving

Holiday gifts, crafted with love, are the best presents to give and the most treasured to receive. Christmas comes but once a year, allowing us the opportunity to show how much we care for someone by giving gifts from our hearts, made by our hands.

Nutcracker

Materials:

- One 10-inch wooden nutcracker
- Small amount of white curly doll hair
- 2 small brass buckles
- 1 decorative button
- 1 gold star
- Scraps of Christmas fabric in plums, blues and greens
- Moss green, dark green, teal, royal purple, burnt orange, royal blue and red acrylic paint
- Black slick paint
- Flat brush
- Fine-line brush
- Pinking shears
- Glue gun/glue sticks

Allow each paint to dry completely before proceeding to the next color.

Step 1

Using fine-line brush and moss green paint, paint outer edges of nutcracker base, top half of legs, belt and brim of cap. Using fine-line brush and red paint, paint upper outer edge of base, sleeves and body of jacket and top of hat. With fine-line brush and dark green paint, paint top of base. Add a few streaks of teal paint to the top.

Step 2

With flat brush and purple paint, paint shoes and jacket cuffs. With flat brush and burnt orange paint, paint bottom half of legs and top of shoulders (epaulets). Using black slick paint, dot buttons on sides of knickers, below belt and on cuffs. Mix red paint with a small amount of water and paint cheeks. Paint eyes royal blue.

Step 3

Using hot glue, attach buckles to shoes. Secure doll hair thickly to head and lower jaw. Use a few strands to form a mustache. Cut a ½ inch band of Christmas fabric and secure to base of hat. Cut smaller strips and secure around legs below knickers. With hot glue, attach button to belt. Attach gold star to front of hat over fabric.

Shadowbox Gifts and Ornaments

Decoupage Ornament

Materials:

❖ One 2½-inch-diameter plastic foam ball
❖ 1 sheet of Christmas wrapping paper
❖ Round brush
❖ Acrylic high-gloss varnish
❖ 1 large brass bell
❖ 10 tiny brass bells
❖ 5 inches of ¼-inch-wide red satin ribbon
❖ 3 red ribbon roses with leaves
❖ White craft glue
❖ Scissors
❖ Glue gun/glue sticks

Step 1

Cut out approximately 30 small holiday motifs from wrapping paper. Working with one paper piece at a time, apply craft glue to the back of each paper piece. Smooth onto ball, overlapping pieces to cover all areas. Allow glue to dry.

Step 2

Use round brush to apply 5 even coats of gloss varnish. Allow varnish to dry completely between coats.

Step 3

To form a hanger, with hot glue secure ends of ribbon to top of ornament. With hot glue attach ribbon roses around loop. Attach large bell to opposite end of the ball. Secure tiny bells around larger bell.

Painted Rocking Horse

Materials:

❖ One 9x6-inch wooden rocking horse
❖ 1 small white porcelain flower
❖ Red, dark moss green, light gray, dark gray and mustard acrylic paint
❖ Flat brush
❖ Fine-line brush
❖ Glue gun/glue sticks

Step 1

Using flat brush and light gray acrylic paint, paint body of horse. Allow paint to dry completely. With flat brush and dark gray paint, paint mane, eyes, tail and hooves. Brush dots of paint on horse for a spotted appearance. Allow paint to dry completely.

Step 2

Using flat brush and red paint, paint saddle and rockers. Allow paint to dry completely.

Step 3

Mix green paint with an equal amount of water. Using fine-line brush, lightly brush on a small amount of wash around saddle, bridle and horse body. Allow paint to dry completely. With hot glue, attach porcelain flower to bridle.

Brett
1993

Materials:

- One 8-inch-diameter clear glass dessert plate
- 1 photograph
- 22 to 25 small designs cut from Christmas gift-wrap
- Acrylic gloss medium
- Metallic green and forest green acrylic paint
- Round brush
- Fine-line black waterproof pen
- Tracing paper
- Pen
- Scissors
- White paper
- Natural sea sponge

Step 1

Turn plate upside down on sheet of white paper. Use brush to apply a coat of gloss medium to front side of one design. Place coated side of design onto plate. Follow this procedure to create a circle around rim of plate, and a wreath shape around plate center.

Step 2

Trim photograph to a circular shape, centering face. Photo edges should overlap paper wreath. Use brush to apply an even coat of gloss medium to front of photograph. Smooth in place. Allow medium to dry approximately 20 minutes.

Step 3

Cut out a pretty shape from white paper. Use permanent pen to add name, date or a message. Allow ink to dry. Apply gloss medium to front of paper. Smooth in place on plate rim beneath photograph.

Step 4

Apply an even coat of gloss medium over entire back of plate. Cover photograph back and paper pieces. Allow to dry completely.

Step 5

Use sponge and metallic green paint to apply a pattern to back of plate. Allow paint to dry completely. Use brush to apply 2 even coats of forest green paint. Allow paint to dry completely between coats.

Step 6

Apply a final coat of gloss medium to back of plate. Allow plate to dry completely.

This plate is for decorative purposes only.

Tin Christmas Plate and Mug

Materials:

For one set:
- ❖ One tin plate
- ❖ One tin mug
- ❖ Blue and white nontoxic opaque paint markers
- ❖ Nail polish remover
- ❖ Cotton swabs
- ❖ Vinegar
- ❖ White paper, cut to plate size
- ❖ Scissors

Step 1

Wash plate and mug in hot soapy water. Rinse in a mixture of ¼ cup vinegar and ¾ cup of water.

Step 2

Practice making a freehand snowman several times on sheets of paper. Using opaque paint markers, re-create design on plate and mug. Any mistakes can be removed with a cotton swab soaked in nail polish remover. Allow paint to dry completely.

This plate is not dishwasher-safe and is for decorative purposes only.

Snowman Doll

Materials:

- ⅓ yard of white terry cloth fabric
- 10 small black pom-poms
- 1 tiny dried chile pepper
- One 2x16-inch piece of plaid wool fabric with fringed ends
- One ¼x9-inch strip of plaid wool fabric
- One 8x8-inch square of gray felt
- 2 sprigs preserved cedar
- 9 tiny brass bells
- 8 inches of ¼-inch-wide red satin ribbon
- Cotton batting
- Graph paper
- Pen
- Black fabric marker
- Straight pins
- Scissors
- Iron
- White thread and needle
- Glue gun/glue sticks

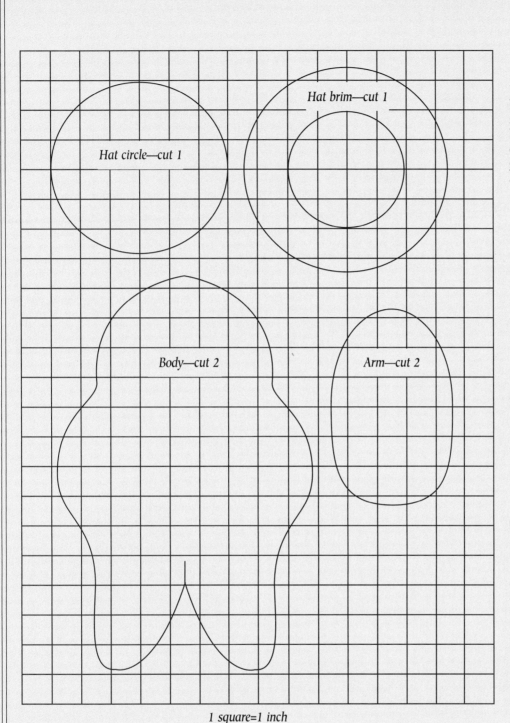

Hat brim—cut 1

Hat circle—cut 1

Body—cut 2

Arm—cut 2

1 square=1 inch

Step 4

Use batting to stuff snowman's body and head firmly. Slip-stitch opening closed. Stuff both arms firmly and slip-stitch openings closed. Using hot glue, attach arms to body at shoulder.

Step 5

Using hot glue, add two pom-poms for snowman's eyes, five pom-poms for a smile and three pom-poms for buttons. Use pepper as a nose. Set snowman aside.

Step 6

Pin hat pattern pieces to gray felt and cut out. Using hot glue, attach hat circle to brim circle. Gather hat circle edges as needed while gluing.

Step 7

Bend one cedar twig to form a circle. Secure ends together with hot glue. Using ribbon, make a small bow (see page 154). Attach bow to twig wreath. Secure bells around wreath. Using hot glue, attach wreath to snowman's right hand. Attach hands to body front. Tuck remaining sprig of cedar in snowman's arm.

Step 1

Use graph paper and pen to enlarge body, arm and hat patterns to full size (see above). Cut out patterns. Set hat pattern aside.

Step 2

Fold terry cloth in half. Pin body pattern and arm pattern to cloth and cut out 2 body pieces and 2 arm pieces. Place body pieces with right sides together. Using a ¼-inch seam allowance, stitch pieces together, leaving a 3-inch opening at top of head. Turn body right side out. Press with cool iron.

Step 3

Fold each arm piece in half lengthwise, with right sides together and edges aligned. Using a ¼-inch seam allowance, sew edges together, leaving top end of each arm open. Turn arms right side out and press.

Small Cardinal Box

Materials:

- One 4¼x2¼-inch round wooden box with lid
- 24½ inches of 1½-inch-wide Christmas tartan ribbon, cut into 14½-inch and 10-inch pieces
- 14½ inches of ¼-inch-wide dark green satin ribbon
- 14½ inches of ¼-inch-wide red-and-gold braid
- Dark green and cardinal red acrylic paint
- Round brush
- 2 small artificial cardinals
- 2 small pinecones
- 2 small red berries
- 4 or 5 sprigs of greenery
- 1 piece of dark green or red felt
- Glue gun/glue sticks

Step 1

Paint top surface of box lid and sides of box bottom with dark green paint. Allow paint to dry before proceeding. Paint edge of lid with red paint. Allow paint to dry completely.

Step 2

Using the 10-inch length of tartan ribbon, make a small bow (see page154). Set aside. Using hot glue, attach the remaining tartan ribbon around sides of box, ½ inch down from rim. A narrow band of green should show at the bottom of box.

Step 3

Using hot glue, secure green satin ribbon around sides of lid, ⅛ inch down from top. Attach red-and-gold braid to sides of lid, just below green ribbon.

Step 4

Using hot glue, attach greenery to center of lid. Add berries, pinecones and cardinals. Glue bow to one side of greenery.

Christmas Tartan Box

Materials:

- One 11¼x9x4-inch oval wooden box with lid
- ½ yard of red-and-green woven tartan fabric
- Fusible sheets to cover box lid, bottom and side areas
- 1 yard of ¾-inch-wide red-and-green woven tartan ribbon
- 2¼ yards of ¼-inch-wide red-and-gold braided trim
- Permanent marker
- Measuring tape
- Pencil
- Ruler
- Scissors
- Iron
- Glue gun/glue sticks

Step 1

Place box lid upside down on fusible sheet. Use pencil to draw around oval. Follow this procedure for box bottom. Place box lid onto box. With pencil, draw a line on box around bottom edge of box lid. Remove lid. Measure the surface on box to be covered with fabric, omitting the area above pencil line. Draw this rectangular shape on fusing material. Cut out.

Step 2

Using heat setting appropriate for tartan fabric and following manufacturer's directions, iron fusing shapes to fabric. Cut out. Remove backing paper from fusing material. Iron pieces in place on box surfaces.

Step 3

Using hot glue, attach ribbon around box lid side. Overlap ribbon ends and trim excess.

Step 4

Using hot glue, attach braided trim around bottom edge of box lid. Trim and secure ends with glue to prevent fraying. Use remaining trim to encircle top edge of box lid. Finish with two loops and a circle. Tuck end behind loop and secure in place with hot glue.

Christmas Bear

Materials:

- ½ yard of honey-colored artificial fur or wool
- 4x8-inch piece of suede or suede-look for paws and soles of feet
- 3x3-inch square of black leather for nose
- ¾ yard of 2-inch-wide red ribbon
- 1½ x¾-inch plastic snap-on nose
- Two 12-millimeter plastic snap-on eyes
- Four 30-millimeter plastic joints
- 1 yard of black yarn
- 1 bag of cotton batting
- Extra strong honey-colored thread and large needle
- Tracing paper
- Straight pins
- Scissors
- Craft knife
- White craft glue
- Glue gun/glue sticks

Step 1

Enlarge patterns to full size and cut out (see pages 88-90). Place fabric, right side down, nap running down, on flat work surface. Pin pattern pieces to wrong side of fabric. Cut out. Where multiples are indicated, turn the pattern piece over and trace its reverse.

Step 2

To form the head, pin wrong sides of fabric together and stitch the 2 side head pieces from the nose point to the neck point. Pin and sew center head piece into the 2 stitched side head pieces.

Step 3

Turn head right side out. Place eyes near each center seam and at curve of snout. Push stems of eyes through fabric. Secure with fasteners. Smooth craft glue over plastic nose. Wrap leather piece around and behind it. Use hot glue to secure leather behind nose. Push nose stem through fabric just above seam. Secure with fastener.

Step 4

To make mouth, thread needle with black yarn. Pierce fabric at center seam, 1 inch from nose. Bring yarn straight up and pierce fabric again at nose. Pull yarn through. Bring needle up to the left of starting point. Pass needle through the bottom of first stitch and down to the right. This will make a line even with the left side.

Step 5

Use batting to stuff head. Insert one joint into the neck, disc side in. Gather fabric around joint, using needle threaded with extra strong thread. Knot off. Wrap thread around twice and knot off again.

Step 6

Stitch ears, right sides together. Leave opening at bottom. Turn ears right side out. Turn bottom edges in. Slip-stitch openings closed. Pin ears into place on seams. Blindstitch into place.

Step 7

Position leg pieces together in pairs, right sides together. Stitch together, leaving openings at bottom and mid-calf. Pin sole to bottom of leg and stitch in place. Clip curves. Repeat for second leg. Turn legs right side out. Insert joint at * (see page 90). Make a tiny hole with tip of craft knife to force the stem through. Be sure that leg joint stems face opposite directions. Stuff legs with cotton batting. Slip-stitch openings closed.

Step 8

Stitch paw to bottom of inside arm piece. Position both arm pieces, right sides together. Stitch outside arm piece to inner arm piece. Leave an opening (see page 88). Turn arms right side out. Insert joints at * (see page 88) through inner arm. Stuff arm and slip-stitch opening closed. Repeat for second arm.

Step 9

Stitch dart in each body piece and clip. Position body pieces, right sides together. Stitch together, leaving an opening at top and lower back. Use extra-strong thread to gather neck opening closed. Knot off. Turn body right side out.

Step 10

With tip of craft knife, make a tiny hole at each * in order to insert joint stems. Push stem of one arm joint through an armhole into the body. In the body, put the washer on the stem. Push pieces together tightly. Repeat this process for remaining arm and legs.

Step 11

Insert head joint stem into gathered neck opening. Put washer on and snap together tightly. Stuff body with cotton batting. Slip-stitch openings closed.

Step 12

With a sewing needle, carefully pick fur from seams. Trim fur around eyes, if necessary. Tie a piece of favorite ribbon in a pretty bow around bear's neck.

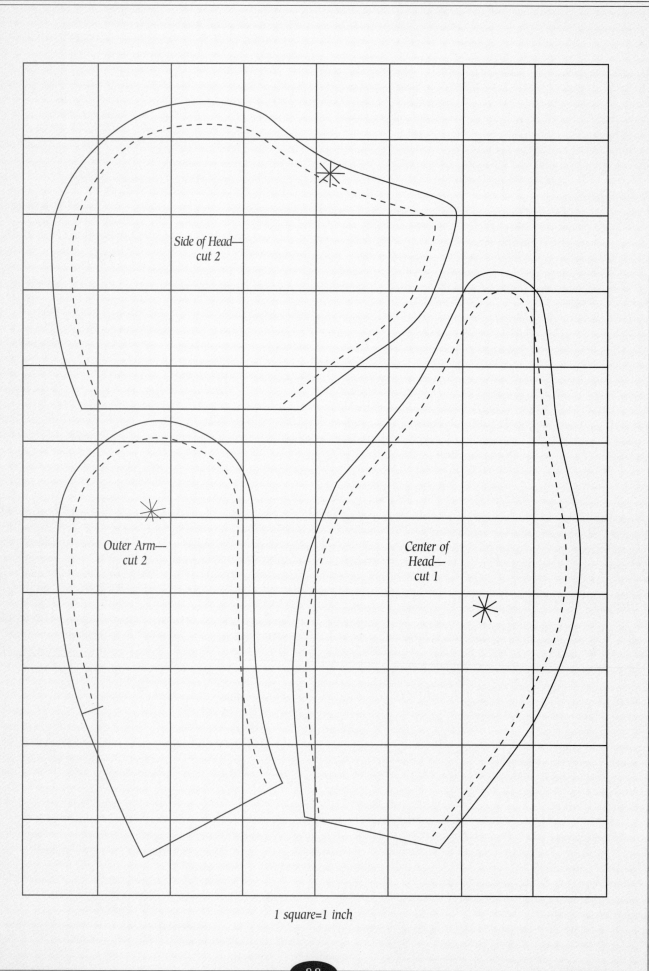

Side of Head—
cut 2

Outer Arm—
cut 2

Center of
Head—
cut 1

1 square=1 inch

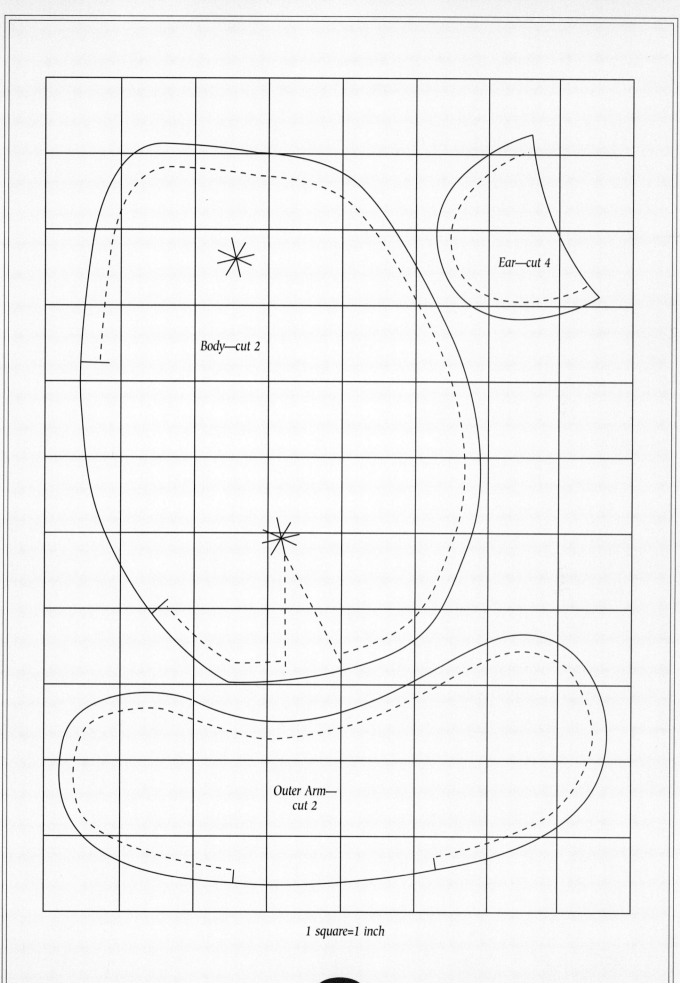

Ear—cut 4

Body—cut 2

Outer Arm—
cut 2

1 square=1 inch

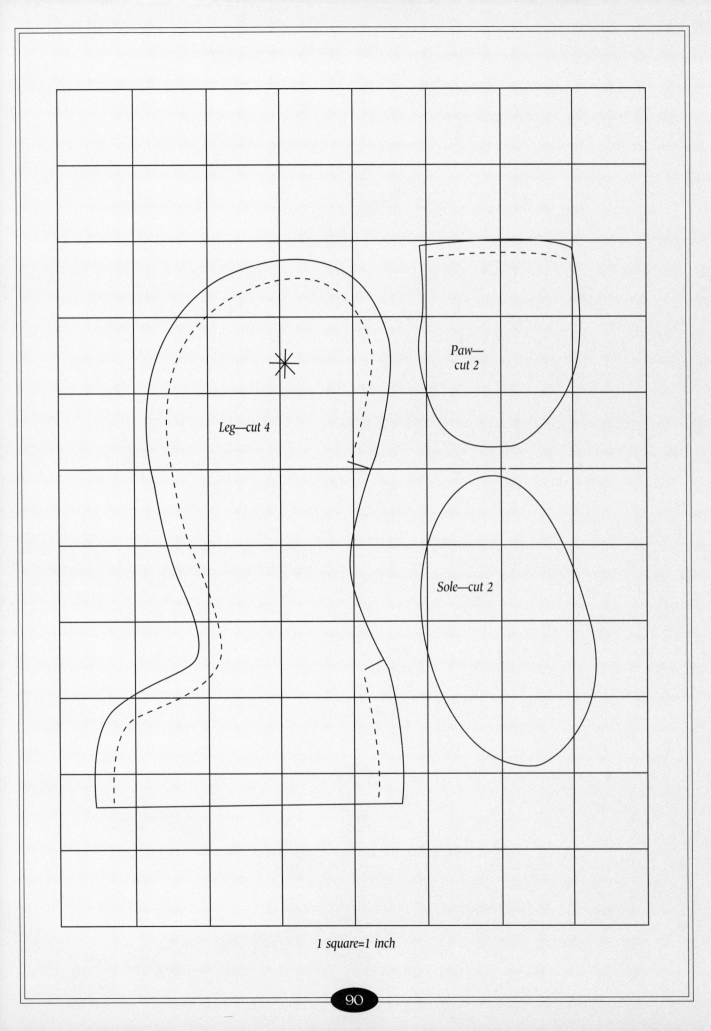

1 square=1 inch

Paw—
cut 2

Leg—cut 4

Sole—cut 2

Three-Piece Scarf Set

Materials:

Yarn used is Heilo 100% Norwegian Wool, Sport Weight, 104 yards per skein.

- ❖ 2 skeins Orange, No. 3418
- ❖ 1 skein Rust/Red, No. 3918
- ❖ 1 skein Green, No. 7562
- ❖ 9 skeins Peacock, No. 7336
- ❖ 1 skein Black, No. 0090
- ❖ 1 skein Gold, No. 828
- ❖ 1 skein White, No. 0010
- ❖ Nylon reinforcement yarn (optional)
- ❖ Knitting elastic (optional)
- ❖ One 11½-inch circular needle, size 4 (for scarf, socks and mittens)
- ❖ One 11½-inch circular needle, size 3 (for socks)
- ❖ One 16-inch circular needle, size 3 (for hat)
- ❖ One set of 5 double-pointed needles, size 3 (for hat)
- ❖ One set of 5 double-pointed needles, size 2 (for mittens and socks)
- ❖ Markers
- ❖ Stitch holder
- ❖ Clover pom-pom maker in 1-inch and 1½-inch sizes

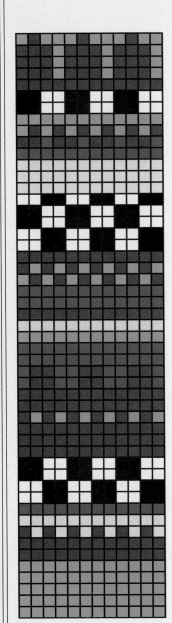

See page 20 for the abbreviations of the terms used in this project.

Gauge: 6 stitches = 1 inch; 8 rounds = 1 inch

N.B.: Nylon reinforcement yarn for the heels and toes is a product that is very hard to find, so Heilo is a good choice. It is very strong and has been Norway's most popular yarn for the last 50 years. Socks made from it do not require reinforcement yarn.

If desired, elastic may be threaded through the wrong side of ankle ribbing or knit along with yarn while working ankle ribbing.

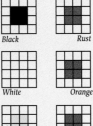

Mitten Dec Rnds		Blue
Black		Rust
White		Orange
Gold		Green

Gauge: 6 stitches = 1 inch on size 4 needle. 8 stitches = 1 inch on size 2 needle

Step 1

To form the mitten cuff, use the blue yarn and cast on 72 sts. Join and place marker.

Round 1-2: Purl. Work the chart (see left) backward, beginning with 51 st round. Decrease 4 sts, evenly spaced on Rounds 40, 29 and 16; 60 sts remain. End off all colors when Round 7 has been completed.

Step 2

To form the mitten, use the double-pointed needles and blue yarn.

Round 1: Knit 15 stitches with each needle.

Round 2: Knit decreasing 1 st in center of each needle. 56 sts remain.

Rounds 3-7: Work in k 1, p 1, ribbing.

Knit 22 rounds even.

Step 3

For the right thumb marking round, knit across the first 2 needles. On needle 3, knit 2 stitches. With waste yarn knit next 10 sts, slide these 10 sts back to left needle and knit again with blue. Knit to end of round. End off waste yarn.

Mittens

Waste yarn will be removed and thumb worked later.

Step 4

Continue to knit around even on 56 sts until mitten is 1½ inches less than desired length.

Step 5

For the mitten decrease:

Round 1: * K 5, k 2 tog, repeat from * around.

Round 2: Knit.

Round 3: * K 4, k 2 tog, repeat from * around.

Round 4: Knit.

Repeat last 2 rounds, with 1 less stitch between decreases each decrease round, until 16 sts remain.

Next round: *K 2 tog, repeat from * around; 8 sts remain. End off yarn, leaving an 8-inch tail. Thread tapestry needle with tail and run through remaining 8 sts. Pull up tightly and secure. Bury end on wrong side.

Step 6

To complete thumb, remove waste yarn. Pick up open loops at top of thumb opening with one double-pointed needle. Pick up open loops at bottom of thumb opening with another double-pointed needle. Pick up 2 sts between needles at each side (24 sts). Knit 6 sts onto each of 4 needles.

Round 1: K 4, sl 1, k 1, psso, k 2 tog, k to end of round.

Rounds 2-5: Knit.

Round 6: K 3, sl 1, k 1, psso, k 2 tog, k to end of round.

Round 7: K 4, knit one more st with first needle, knit the next 5 sts with needle No. 2. Knit 5 sts with needle No. 3, knit last 5 sts with needle No. 4. Each needle now contains 5 sts.

Continue to knit even on until thumb is ½ inch less than desired length.

Step 7

For the thumb decrease:

Round 1: K 2 tog, around. 10 sts.

Round 2: Knit.

Repeat decrease round; 5 sts remain. End off yarn, leaving an 8-inch tail. Thread tapestry needle with tail. Run tail through remaining 5 sts. Pull up tightly and secure. Bury end on wrong side.

Step 8

Repeat for second mitten up to the right thumb marking round.

Step 9

For the left thumb marking round use blue yarn and knit across first needle. Knit across 2 sts from needle No. 2. With waste yarn knit next 10 sts on needle No. 2. Slide these same 10 sts back onto left needle. With blue yarn, knit the 10 sts in waste yarn and last 2 sts remaining on needle No. 2. Knit to end of round.

Step 10

Finish left mitten as for right mitten.

Hat

Step 1

With waste yarn cast on 132 stitches. End off waste yarn.

Round 1: Knit with blue yarn. Join and place marker. Work chart (see left page) beginning with Round 7. Complete chart. End off all colors but blue.

Step 2

Knit around with main color, decreasing 4 sts evenly spaced. This leaves 128 sts.

Step 3

To form the crown, change to the double-pointed needles. Cast on 32 sts on each needle.

Round 1: *Knit 14, k 2 tog, repeat from * around.

Round 2: *Knit 13, k 2 tog, repeat from * around.

Repeat decrease round with one less st between decreases until each needle has 2 sts.

Step 4

End off yarn and leave a 10-inch tail. Thread tapestry needle with tail. Run tail through remaining 8 sts. Pull tail up tightly and secure. Bury end on wrong side.

Step 5

Turn hat upside down. Using circular size 3 knitting needle, pick up loops of first blue round. Remove waste yarn. With blue work 3 rounds k 1, p 1 of ribbing.

Step 6

Bind off 34 sts for back of neck. Knit across 20 sts for right earflap. Place on holder to be worked later.

Bind off 58 sts for front of hat. Knit across 20 sts for left earflap.

Step 7

To form left earflap:

Rows 1-7: Sl 1, knit to end.

Rows 8-11: Sl 1, k 2 tog, k to last 3 sts, sl 1, k 1, psso, k 1; 12 sts remain. Repeat Row 1 on remaining 12 sts until earflap measures 2 inches from beginning. Repeat Row 8 until 4 sts remain. Bind off 4 sts. End off yarn and bury end.

Step 8

Pick up stitches of right earflap and repeat directions for left earflap.

Step 9

Using clover pom-pom maker, make 2 multi-colored 1 ½-inch pom-poms and 4 multi-colored 1-inch pom-poms. Sew 2 small and 1 large pom-poms on each earflap. Make 1 blue 1 ½-inch pom-pom for top of hat.

Scarf

Finished size of scarf is 54x6 inches.

Step 1

Using Peacock (blue) yarn, cast on 72 stitches. Join and place marker.

Round 1-2: Purl.

Knit 51 rounds of chart (see left page). End off all contrast colors.

Step 2

With blue yarn, knit until piece measures 46 inches from cast-on stitches. Knit 51 rounds of chart (see left page) backward to first round. Purl 2 rounds and bind off. Steam scarf.

Step 3

Using clover pom-pom maker, make 6 multi-colored 1½-inch pom-poms for scarf. Sew 3 on each end by tying the pom-poms through the double thickness of scarf.

Christmas Jewelry

Ribbon Rose Button Cover

Materials:

❖ 12 inches of 1-inch-wide deep red satin wire-edged ribbon
❖ 16 inches of 1½-inch-wide deep green satin wire-edged ribbon
❖ 13 inches of ½-inch-wide variegated organdy ribbon with gold edge
❖ 1 button cover back
❖ Glue gun/glue sticks

Step 1

Use red ribbon to make a ruffled rose by folding one end of ribbon over on itself and pressing wire bends in place. Gently work wire from opposite end free. Push ribbon along wire to create a ruffle. Place a small dot of glue on wire at end of ruffle to secure in place. Begin at folded end and wind ruffled edge around itself until a rose is formed. Secure in place by winding extended wire around rose base several times.

Step 2

Use green ribbon to make a ruffled piece 8 inches long. Form 2 loops with this piece. Secure loops by winding extended wire around center. Pinch loop ends to resemble leaves.

Step 3

Using organdy ribbon, form a small triple bow with 2-inch streamers (see page 155). Using hot glue, attach this bow to green leaves. Secure rose to center of organdy bow. Secure button cover back to green leaves.

Holiday Button Pin

Materials:

❖ One 1⅜-inch blank button form
❖ Scraps of red Christmas-print fabric
❖ 1 yard of 1½-inch-wide metallic gold mesh wire-edged ribbon
❖ Small pin back
❖ Glue gun/glue sticks

Step 1

Follow button blank manufacturer's instructions to cover button with fabric.

Step 2

Twist gold ribbon length tightly. Twisted length will begin to form loops as you continue to twist. With hot glue, attach ribbon loops around front of button. Secure ribbon ends to back of button. With hot glue attach pin back to button.

Christmas Bells Pin

Materials:

- One 2½-inch adhesive-backed foam-covered oval form
- 4x4-inch square of Christmas-print fabric
- ¾ yard of ⅛-inch-wide red satin ribbon
- One 1¾-inch bells-and-holly brass charm
- 3 small brass bells
- 8 inches of ¼-inch-wide metallic gold braided trim
- Scissors
- Glue gun/glue sticks

Step 1

Follow manufacturer's instructions to cover oval with fabric piece.

Step 2

Use hot glue to attach braided trim around outer edge of oval.

Step 3

Cut one 3½-inch piece from red ribbon. Set aside. Use remaining ribbon to make a triple bow, 2 inches wide overall, with 3 streamers (see page 155). Tie a brass bell to each streamer. Secure each knot with a dot of hot glue. Trim excess ribbon. Tie brass charm on 3½-inch length. Using hot glue, secure the opposite end of ribbon to bow center. Attach bow to center of oval.

Gold Bow Pin

Materials:

- 21 inches of 1½-inch-wide metallic gold mesh wire-edged ribbon
- One ⅝-inch gold button with rhinestones
- Pin back
- Glue gun/glue sticks

Step 1

Cut 7 inches of ribbon and set piece aside. Fold one end of remaining ribbon over onto itself, pressing wire bends to secure. Work one wire free from opposite end. Push ribbon along wire to gather tightly. Form a ruffled circle by pinching gathered area together. Secure with hot glue. Secure ribbon ends together with hot glue.

Step 2

Form a small bow with remaining ribbon (see page 154). Using hot glue, attach bow to center of ruffled circle. Secure button to bow center. Attach pin back to back of ruffled circle.

Tasseled Button Cover

Materials:

- One 1¼-inch blank button form
- Scrap deep green satin
- One ⅝-inch gold button with rhinestone
- One 1-inch burgundy tassel
- 1 button cover form
- Glue gun/glue sticks

Step 1

Follow the button cover manufacturer's instructions to cover button form with fabric scrap.

Step 2

Using hot glue, attach top end of tassel to center of button. Secure gold button to top of tassel.

Step 3

Attach button cover form to back of button with hot glue.

Christmas Cherub Pin

Materials:

- One 2½-inch adhesive-backed foam-covered oval form
- One 2-inch brass cherub charm
- ¾ yard thin metallic gold elastic cord
- 8 inches of ¼-inch metallic gold braided trim with red accents
- 4x4-inch square of Christmas-print fabric
- Pin back
- Glue gun/glue sticks

Step 1

Follow manufacturer's instructions to cover oval with fabric.

Step 2

Using hot glue, attach braided trim around outer edge of oval.

Step 3

Using gold cord, form a bow approximately 2 inches wide overall with many loops (see page 155). Secure bow over center with hot glue. Attach charm to bow center. Attach pin back to reverse side of oval form. Arrange bow loops in a fan position.

Child's Christmas Stool

Materials:

- 11½x8½x8½-inch wooden stool with four legs
- Deep red and pine green acrylic paint
- Acrylic low-luster varnish
- Assorted Christmas stickers
- Assorted Christmas wrapping paper
- 1-inch flat brush
- Round brush
- Sharp scissors

Step 1

Using brush and green paint, paint entire stool with 2 coats. Allow paint to dry completely between coats.

Step 2

Cut out approximately 30 Santa, toy, children and ornament motifs from wrapping paper. These designs will be supplemented with 4 or 5 Christmas stickers.

Step 3

Work with one paper piece at a time. Use flat brush to apply a coat of acrylic varnish to back of paper piece. Place paper on stool top. Continue to affix pieces to stool edge. Leave center section open. Add a sticker and small designs to stool front. Stickers may be placed without the use of acrylic varnish. Allow varnish to dry approximately 20 minutes.

Step 4

Use round brush to paint upper and lower turnings of stool legs red. Paint top of stool red, leaving approximately ⅛ inch of green paint exposed around each paper design. Allow paint to dry completely. Apply a second coat of red if coverage is not complete. Allow paint to dry completely.

Step 5

Using round brush, apply 3 coats of acrylic varnish to entire stool. Allow varnish to dry completely between coats.

Christmas Door Bells

Materials:

- ❖ 2 large artificial green boughs
- ❖ Three 4- or 5-inch pinecones
- ❖ One 2½-inch brass bell
- ❖ One 2-inch brass bell
- ❖ Two 1½-inch brass bells
- ❖ 3 small brass bells
- ❖ 3 small sprigs artificial ivy
- ❖ 6 artificial red berry picks, with 5 berries on each pick
- ❖ 2⅔ yards of 1¼-inch-wide red, green and gold plaid ribbon
- ❖ 2 yards of 2½-inch-wide red wire-edged moiré ribbon
- ❖ 5 ⅓ yards of ¼-inch-wide red satin ribbon
- ❖ Scissors
- ❖ Florist's wire
- ❖ Wire cutter
- ❖ Glue gun/glue sticks

Step 1

With florist's wire, attach pine boughs together for a total length of approximately 30 inches. Cut off 20 inches of red wire-edged ribbon. Set aside. Cut 6 feet of plaid ribbon. Place plaid ribbon on top of remaining moiré ribbon. Make a large triple bow using both ribbons (see page 155). Secure bow center with a twist of wire.

Step 2

Center bow on 20-inch length of red wire-edged ribbon. Use hot glue every 3 to 4 inches to secure bow to moiré ribbon. Use a twist of florist's wire to secure bow center to ribbon center. Wire bow and ribbon to greenery.

Step 3

Finish streamer ends in an inverted "V" shape and arrange as desired. Secure with hot glue.

Step 4

Cut red satin ribbon into 7 equal lengths. Thread a bell onto each ribbon length. Knot at top. Gather ribbons together with bells at different lengths, with the largest bell on the shortest ribbon and the smallest bell on the longest ribbon. Tie all ribbons together. Use hot glue to secure knot to greenery, just below bow.

Step 5

Use wire to secure pinecones to boughs, distributing evenly. Use hot glue to secure berry picks to greenery, distributing evenly. Attach sprigs of ivy down the center of arrangement.

Step 6

Cut remaining 4 feet of plaid ribbon into 4 equal lengths to use as streamers. Finish streamer ends in an inverted "V" shape. Wind ribbons through greenery and secure in place with hot glue. To form a hanger, cut 8 inches of florist's wire. Fold the wire in half and thread through the back of boughs. Twist wire ends together to form a loop.

Christmas Photo Holders

Festive Photo Frame

Materials:

- One 5x7-inch finished wood frame
- 1 precut mat, 5x7-inch outside edge, 4½x3-inch inside cutout
- 7x8½-inch piece holly-print fabric
- 2x8-inch piece of fabric, red with small white dots, cut into four 2-inch squares
- 12 inches of 1⅛-inch-wide green satin ribbon, cut into 3-inch pieces
- Scissors
- Craft knife
- Spray adhesive
- Iron
- Glue gun/glue sticks

Step 1

Working in a well-ventilated area, cover face of mat with spray adhesive. Allow to dry for 30 seconds. Center and position facedown on wrong side of holly-print fabric. Smooth fabric with fingers to eliminate air bubbles and wrinkles.

Step 2

With the craft knife, carefully cut an X into the fabric, allowing 3/4 inch from all 4 inside corners. Trim away center. Fold over excess and secure in place with hot glue.

Step 3

Fold dotted fabric squares into triangles. Press with warm iron. Use hot glue to secure triangles into place on corners of mat face. Fold raw edges over mat edge and secure to back of mat with hot glue.

Step 4

Use hot glue to secure ribbon pieces along folded edge of dotted fabric. Fold ends over edge of mat and secure in place with hot glue. Place finished mat against glass in frame.

Holiday Photo Frame

Materials:

- 1 precut mat, 5x7-inch outside edge, 3x4-inch inside cutout
- 6½x8½-inch piece red-and-green plaid fabric
- 1½ yards of ¹⁄₁₆-inch-wide red cord
- 5x7-inch piece of ¹⁄₁₆-inch cardboard
- 4x4-inch piece of ¹⁄₁₆-inch cardboard
- Scissors
- Craft knife
- Tracing paper
- Spray adhesive
- Glue gun/glue sticks

Step 1

Working in a well-ventilated area, apply spray adhesive to wrong side of plaid fabric and precut mat face. Allow to dry for 30 seconds. Center and position mat facedown on fabric. Smooth fabric with fingers to eliminate air bubbles and wrinkles.

Step 2

Fold fabric corners onto back of mat. Secure in place with hot glue. Pull side pieces of fabric around mat. Secure in place with hot glue.

Step 3

Using craft knife, slit fabric at center of mat. Trim fabric, allowing ½ inch from all edges. Fold fabric onto back of mat and secure with hot glue.

Step 4

Turn frame so right side is facing up. With hot glue, attach red cord around outer and inner edges. Trim excess. Turn cord ends to back and secure with hot glue.

Step 5

Cut an 8½-inch piece of cord. Make a double knot in one end. Using hot glue, secure the unknotted end to the frame at center, just above the top inner edge. Form 3 loops of equal size, left, center and right. Secure in place with hot glue. Secure double knot into center of loops with glue.

Step 6

With hot glue, attach the 5x7-inch cardboard piece to back of mat. Leave bottom open so photograph may be placed inside.

Covered Small Photo Album

Materials:

- One 5x7-inch paper-covered photo album
- 16x6-inch piece of red-and-green lattice-with-ivy fabric
- 1 yard of ⅞-inch-wide ruffled ribbon
- 1¼ yards of ¹⁄₁₆-inch-wide red cord (a small amount of clear tape will keep ends from unraveling)
- Two 4½x6¼-inch pieces green or red card stock
- Scissors
- Spray adhesive
- Glue gun/glue sticks

Step 1

Working in a well-ventilated area, cover wrong side of fabric with spray adhesive. Center and press fabric against photo album cover. There should be ½ inch of excess fabric to fold over edges. Smooth fabric with fingers to remove any air bubbles or wrinkles.

Step 2

Fold corners over onto inside of cover, forming a triangle. Secure in place with hot glue. Fold remaining edges over onto inside of cover. Secure in place with hot glue.

Step 3

Use hot glue to secure ruffle to entire inside edge of cover. Use hot glue to attach red cord onto outside edge of album. Trim excess.

Step 4

Use remaining cord to form 3 loops of equal size, left, center and right. With hot glue, secure loops to front center edge of album. Trim excess. Use cord to form a double knot. Secure knot into center of loops with hot glue.

Step 5

Using hot glue, secure card stock to the inside of front and back covers to hide raw edges and give album a finished look.

Christmas Video Cover

Materials:

- ❖ 1 plastic videotape container
- ❖ 11½x8½-inch piece of Christmas fabric green with red bows
- ❖ 1 ⅙ yards of ¹⁄₁₆-inch-wide red cord
- ❖ 16 inches of ⅞-inch-wide green ruffled ribbon
- ❖ ⅔ yard of 1½-inch-wide French wire-edged ribbon, red with green edge
- ❖ 1 brass French horn charm
- ❖ Scissors
- ❖ Spray adhesive
- ❖ Glue gun/glue sticks

Step 1

Working in a well-ventilated area, cover wrong side of fabric and outside of video case with spray adhesive. Allow to dry for 30 seconds. Center and press fabric onto video cover. Smooth with fingers to eliminate any air bubbles or wrinkles. Turn edges of fabric over lip of cover. Press and smooth into place, using hot glue if necessary.

Step 2

Cut 10½ inches of wire-edged ribbon. Position ribbon diagonally across face of cover. Secure in place with hot glue. Make a single bow with remaining ribbon (see page 154). Use hot glue to attach bow to diagonal ribbon. Attach French horn to bow. Finish streamer ends in an inverted "V" shape.

Step 3

Use hot glue to secure red cord to extreme edge of covered holder. Trim cord. Attach ruffled ribbon ¹⁄₁₆-inch below lip of bottom of video cover.

Stenciled Desk Set

Materials:

- 1 blank canvas desk set: pencil holder, notepaper holder and letter holder
- Light forest green, dark forest green and red acrylic paint
- 3 sheets clear acetate
- Craft knife or electric stencil cutter
- 1 small sheet glass
- Natural sea sponge
- Masking tape
- Tracing paper
- Pencil

Step 1

Using pencil and tracing paper, trace holly leaf and ivy patterns (on the right). Place traced drawing on a flat surface. Position glass over tracing. Tape acetate corners in place on glass. With craft knife or electric stencil cutter, cut out shapes. Cut one stencil for each holly leaf design.

Step 2

Dip sponge in light green paint. Apply a pattern to blank canvas pieces. Allow paint to dry completely.

Step 3

Hold stencil in position on center portion of a sponged canvas piece. Dip sponge in dark green paint. Sponge dark green paint on leaf areas. Sponge red paint on berry shapes. Remove stencil. Stencil the 4-leaf holly design on letter holder, the 3-leaf design around pencil holder, spacing designs evenly, and the 2-leaf holly design on notepaper holder. Allow paint to dry completely.

Mossed Oval Frame

See photo on page 103

Materials:

- One 4x5-inch oval plastic frame
- Small amount sphagnum moss
- 1 long branch preserved cedar
- 5 small pinecones
- 5 pieces variegated holly
- 3 sprigs preserved miniature baby's breath
- White craft glue
- Glue gun/glue sticks

Step 1

Remove glass from frame. Spread craft glue over frame surface. Cover completely with moss.

Step 2

Cut cedar branch into 5-inch pieces. Secure to frame, overlapping as needed to eliminate gaps. Using hot glue, secure holly in place to the lower left side of frame. Add pinecones, baby's breath and remaining cedar, distributing materials evenly and filling in any gaps.

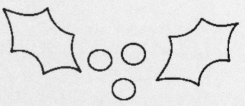

Dear Toni
Thanks so much
for the wonderful
desk set. We just
love it!
Happy Holidays
from Jodee and Dave

Christmas Rose Nosegay

Materials:

- One 7 ½-inch moss green velvet paper nosegay holder
- 7 dried Fire and Ice roses
- 6 to 7 artificial ivy leaves
- 1 spray German statice or sea lavender
- 18 deep red artificial berries
- 1 small bunch preserved cedar
- Handful sphagnum moss
- 1 yard of 1-inch garnet red grosgrain wire-edged ribbon
- Glue gun/glue sticks

Step 1

Using hot glue, secure moss to center area of nosegay holder. Secure one rose to center of mossed area. Attach remaining roses around center rose, facing outward.

Step 2

Using hot glue, secure ivy leaves near roses. Attach remaining botanicals around roses. Place a ring of cedar overlapping onto nosegay holder to frame bouquet. Attach berries in groups of 3, evenly spaced.

Step 3

Make a double bow with streamers (see page 155). Finish streamer ends in an inverted "V" shape. Using hot glue, secure bow to top of nosegay holder, just below cedar.

Christmas Rose Twig Arrangement

Materials:

- One 18½x10-inch Victorian twig wall plaque
- 10 dried Fire and Ice roses
- 10 to 12 artificial grape leaves
- 1 bunch preserved greenery
- Glue gun/glue sticks

Step 1

Using hot glue, secure one rose to lower left-hand corner of twig wall plaque. Attach three artificial leaves behind rose. Encircle rose and leaves with sprigs of greenery, secured in place with hot glue.

Step 2

Place remaining roses in a crescent shape, beginning approximately 4 inches from first rose and ending on the upper right-hand side of plaque. Secure in place with hot glue.

Step 3

Attach remaining leaves and greenery to rose crescent with hot glue. Frame the roses with greens facing outward.

Merry Christmas Box

Materials:

- One 3¼x 12-inch-diameter round wooden box
- 1½-inch wooden letters to spell MERRY CHRISTMAS
- Soft moss green, metallic pale gold and metallic red acrylic paint
- Red and glittery red slick paint
- Ten 1½-inch-long artificial grape leaves
- 2¼ yards of ¾-inch-wide house-patterned woven Christmas ribbon
- ⅓ yard of ¾-inch-wide red grosgrain ribbon with gold metallic stripes
- 1-inch flat brush
- Natural sea sponge
- Glue gun/glue sticks

Step 1

Use flat brush to paint box exterior moss green. Allow paint to dry completely. Dip sponge in gold paint and apply a pattern to box exterior. Allow paint to dry completely.

Step 2

Paint all wooden letters with metallic red paint. Allow paint to dry completely. Use hot glue to attach letters to box lid. Place "Merry" at top of circle, approximately ¼ inch from edge. Space letters evenly. Place "Christmas" around bottom of circle. Space to match lettering at top.

Step 3

Use hot glue to attach leaves to center of box lid in a wreath shape. Use glittery red and red slick paint to paint groupings of three red berries on and around wreath of leaves. Allow paint to dry completely.

Step 4

Cut two 2½-inch pieces from red ribbon. Trim one end of each piece in a point. Secure pieces to top of wreath with points placed downward. Tops should overlap to create streamers. Make a single bow of remaining red ribbon. Attach bow to overlapped top of streamers.

Step 5

Cut length of patterned ribbon in half. Using hot glue, attach one piece around side of lid. Secure remaining ribbon around bottom section of box, approximately ¼ inch from bottom edge.

Children's Crafts

Christmas through the eyes of a child is surely a vision of the season. Chains of colorful paper are crafted by small hands to decorate the tree. Paint, glitter and even a stray mitten can combine to become a jolly puppet in this magical season.

Storybook Glove Puppets

Goldilocks and the Three Bears

Materials:

- ❖ 1 knit glove
- ❖ 1 wooden bead
- ❖ 1 large tan pom-pom
- ❖ 1 medium tan pom-pom
- ❖ 7 small tan pom-poms
- ❖ Small piece printed ribbon
- ❖ Woolly blond doll hair
- ❖ 1 dollhouse bowl
- ❖ Scraps of felt, ribbon and trims
- ❖ Assorted colors of slick paints
- ❖ Low-melt glue gun/glue sticks

Step 1

Assemble baby, mama and papa bear heads by gluing 1 small, 1 medium and 1 large pom-pom to fifth, fourth and third fingers of glove.

Step 2

Glue remaining small pom-poms on for ears. Glue ribbon scrap around forefinger and glue wooden bead on for Goldilocks' head.

Step 3

Glue doll hair to bead. Glue bowl to top of thumb. Glue trims to decorate bears and Goldilocks.

Step 4

Paint faces on bears and Goldilocks and paint dots or designs on glove to decorate. Allow paint to dry completely.

Reindeer

Materials:

- ❖ 1 pair brown wool gloves
- ❖ 2 large tan pom-poms
- ❖ 1 small red pom-pom
- ❖ 5 small black pom-poms
- ❖ 6 small brass bells
- ❖ ¾ yard of ⅛-inch-wide red ribbon
- ❖ ¾ yard of ⅛-inch-wide green ribbon
- ❖ Low-melt glue gun/glue sticks

Step 1

With hot glue attach tan pom-poms to centers of glove tops. To make eyes, glue 2 black pom-poms to glove above tan pom-poms. Glue a black pom-pom nose on 1 reindeer. Glue a red pom-pom nose on the other for a "Rudolph" nose.

Step 2

Cut both ribbon lengths in half. Make 2 small bows, using a red and green ribbon together. Glue bows under tan pom-poms. Glue 3 bells to the center of each bow.

Holly and Poinsettia Dolls

Materials

For holly doll:
- ❖ One 3- or 3½-inch wooden doll form
- ❖ White, red and black acrylic paint
- ❖ 1 stem variegated artificial holly leaves and berries
- ❖ Small amount Spanish moss or doll hair
- ❖ 3 small red ribbon roses with leaves
- ❖ Small paint brush
- ❖ Low-melt glue gun/glue sticks

For poinsettia doll:
- ❖ One 3- or 3½-inch wooden doll form
- ❖ Red and black acrylic paint
- ❖ 4 small artificial red poinsettia flowers
- ❖ 8 to 10 green artificial holly leaves
- ❖ Red (or color of choice) doll hair
- ❖ Small paint brush
- ❖ Low-melt glue gun/glue sticks

Step 1

To paint holly doll, mix a dot of red paint with approximately 1 tablespoon of white paint. Paint doll body and face. Allow paint to dry completely. Poinsettia doll has a natural wood finish. Use red paint and small brush to paint smiles and red cheeks on both dolls. Use black paint dots for their eyes. Allow paint to dry completely.

Step 2

Remove holly leaves and berries from their stems. Separate 2 poinsettia flowers and remove from stems. Using hot glue, form a holly leaf dress with collar to one doll by layering holly leaves starting at the bottom of doll . Glue a poinsettia collar and skirt to the remaining doll. Using hot glue, secure holly leaves around poinsettia doll's waist for a long skirt.

Step 3

Using hot glue, attach hair to both heads. Glue ribbon roses to holly doll's hair. Glue 2 poinsettia flowers to the other doll for a red hat.

Gingerbread House

Materials:

- 1 small square cardboard gift box, bottom only
- 1 sheet brown construction paper
- 1 sheet brown tissue paper
- ½ sheet white poster board
- 1 square red felt
- 6 inches pearl trim
- Slick paints in all colors
- Craft glue
- Brush for applying craft glue
- Scissors
- Pinking shears (optional)
- Ruler
- Pencil

Step 1

Make a roof pattern for your house by laying box side on poster board and drawing around shape. Place box side along 1 line of the square and draw a second square. Draw a line all around double square, ½ inch from outer edges. Use scissors or pinking shears to cut out along outside line. Set roof aside.

Step 2

Lay box side on brown construction or tissue paper. Draw around 1 side 4 times to make the outside walls of the house. Cut out the patterns. Glue these brown shapes to box sides, using craft glue applied with a brush.

Step 3

Fold construction paper in half. Measure one side of box. Use a ruler to draw this measurement on construction paper. This will be the bottom line of a triangular roof brace. Use ruler to draw traingle with lines meeting above the centerpoint of bottom line. Draw 1-inch tab to the bottom line.

Cut out two roof braces. Glue tabs to inside of boxtop opening opposite one another.

Step 4

Fold roof in half. Apply glue to edges of triangle and to roof edges. Place roof on triangles.

Step 5

Cut out a rectangle of red felt to use as a door; top may be rounded if you like. Glue door to front of house. Glue pearls to top of roofline. Decorate house with all colors of paint. Make some large dots of paint and after they have dried, add a tiny red dot for a cherry center. These will look like real candy. You can paint a little tree on the side of the house, or maybe a snowman.

Miniature Christmas Tree

Materials:

- One 9-inch artificial tree with base
- Slick paints in all colors
- Crystal glitter
- Newspaper

Step 1

Place newspaper on flat surface and set tree on newspaper. Squirt dots of paints to decorate tree. Allow paint to dry completely.

Step 2

Place fresh paint dots on top of dried dots for more dimension. While second set of dots is wet, sprinkle on crystal glitter. Allow paint to dry completely.

Step 3

Gently shake excess glitter from tree onto newspaper.

Step 4

Paint a red heart and big green X on tree base to decorate.

Jolly Snowmen

Materials:

- 2 plastic foam balls of graduated size
- 2 toothpicks
- 1 square each red and green felt
- Tracing paper
- Pen
- Glossy black, red, pink and green slick paints
- Scissors
- Trim to decorate: bells, small flowers, ornaments or candy canes
- Crystal glitter (optional)
- Spray glue (optional)
- White craft glue or low-melt glue gun/glue sticks

Step 1

Connect 2 plastic foam balls by piercing one with toothpicks and pushing second ball onto exposed toothpick ends. Secure balls together with craft glue or hot glue.

Step 2

Press larger ball gently on flat surface to make a flat bottom. This will allow your snowman to stand up.

Step 3

Use tracing paper and pen to trace hat and scarf patterns (illustrations 1 and 2). Cut out patterns and draw around them onto red and green felt. Cut out felt hat and scarf, trimming ends of scarf into a fringe. Fold hat shape to form a cone. Secure back with glue and fold up brim. Decorate hat and scarf with paint and trims and set aside.

Step 4

Paint a happy face and buttons on snowman and allow paint to dry completely. Glue on hat and scarf.

Step 5

To add glitter to your snowman, have an adult spray snowman lightly with spray glue in a well-ventilated area. Shake crystal glitter onto snowman.

Scarf

1 square=1 inch
illustration 1

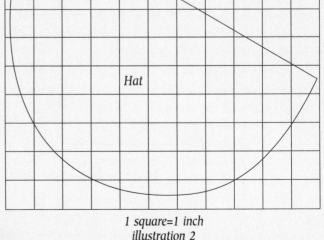

Hat

1 square=1 inch
illustration 2

Christmas Bunny Doll

Materials:

- 1 blank canvas bunny doll
- 1 blank canvas pinafore
- ½ yard of red ruffled ribbon
- 2 black buttons
- 1 black ball button
- 1 red wooden bead
- 2 white ribbon roses
- 1 red ribbon rose
- ½ yard of ¼-inch-wide green satin ribbon
- Red and green slick paints
- Paint brush
- Low-melt glue gun/glue sticks

Step 1

Use red and green paints to decorate bunny's pinafore with dots and holly leaves. Set pinafore aside and allow paint to dry completely.

Step 2

Glue black buttons for bunny's eyes and glue on black ball button for nose.

Step 3

Paint a striped and dotted shirt directly onto bunny's body. Use paint brush to paint little red dancing shoes. Paint a happy smile and heart cheeks with red paint. Allow paint to dry completely.

Step 4

Glue ruffled ribbon around bunny's neck and arms at sleeve lines. Glue red wooden bead just beneath ribbon collar.

Step 5

Cut green ribbon in half and glue each piece to form crossed straps for bunny's shoes.

Step 6

Glue white ribbon roses to bunny's legs and a red ribbon rose just below her ear. Dress bunny in her decorated pinafore.

Christmas Necklace and Bracelet

Materials:

For necklace:
- ❖ 3 glittery gold pipe cleaners
- ❖ 18 red plastic pony beads
- ❖ 16 green plastic pony beads

Step 1

Twist ends of 2 pipe cleaners together. Leave 1 inch of each end extended. Thread 1 green and 1 red bead on each extended end. Fold over ends to secure.

Step 2

Thread the beads, alternating 5 of the red and 4 of the green beads on each side of necklace. Allow gold to show between each bead. Twist ends of remaining pipe cleaners to beaded pipe cleaner ends to form a necklace.

Make a matching bracelet with 1 glittery gold pipe cleaner, 7 green beads and 7 red beads. Thread beads onto pipe cleaner. Twist ends to close.

Smiling Snowman Pin

Materials:

- ❖ One 1 ¼-inch-diameter wooden button
- ❖ One ¾-inch-diameter wooden button
- ❖ Scrap of green Christmas fabric, cut into small triangles
- ❖ 4x ¼-inch scrap of red Christmas fabric for scarf
- ❖ White and teal acrylic paint
- ❖ Fine-line brush
- ❖ Medium green, red and glitter gold slick paint
- ❖ Pin back
- ❖ Glue gun/glue sticks

Step 1

Using fine-line brush, paint button fronts with white paint. Allow paint to dry completely. Using hot glue, attach smaller button to larger, overlapping slightly. This will form the snowman's head and body.

Step 2

Cut green fabric in a small triangle with rounded corners and glue at an angle to snowman's head. Cut red fabric in a 2 ½x¼-inch strip and fringe ends. Glue around the neck to form a scarf.

Step 3

Using fine-line brush and teal paint, dot on eyes and a smiling mouth. Using red slick paint, make little dots around base of snowman's hat and one at the topmost point. Using green slick paint, make buttons. Using gold slick paint, make a nose and decorate the scarf. Use hot glue to attach pin back to snowman's back.

Christmas Bow Pin

Materials:

- 2 red glittery pipe cleaners
- 2 green glittery pipe cleaners
- 1 pin back
- Low-melt glue gun/ glue sticks

Step 1

Twist 1 red and 1 green pipe cleaner together to give a candy cane effect. Repeat with second red and green pipe cleaners.

Step 2

Form a bow using 1 twisted piece. Wrap second twisted piece around bow center. Bend bow loops into a heart-shape. Attach pin back with hot glue.

Decorated Christmas Shoes

Materials:

- One pair children's patent leather shoes
- Two 2¼-inch green satin puffy Christmas trees

- Glittery red, glittery blue, glittery gold, glittery silver, glittery copper, glittery purple and red slick paint
- Low-melt glue gun/glue sticks

Paint dots of all colors on trees to make ornaments. Set trees aside to dry. Paint dots of red and glittery silver around top edge of shoe. Allow paint to dry. Use hot glue to fasten trees to the front of shoes.

Animals Christmas Shirt

Materials:

❖ 1 child's sweatshirt, prewashed to remove sizing
❖ Dark green, yellow, brown, red, crystal, black, orange, glittery green, glittery silver and glittery gold slick paint
❖ Tracing paper
❖ Black or blue fine-line iron-on transfer pen
❖ Iron

Step 1

Place tracing paper on design (see page to right). Use iron-on transfer pen to trace design.

Step 2

Position traced drawing ink side down, on front of shirt. Follow pen manufacturer's instructions for iron setting; cotton setting is usually recommended. Hold paper in place and press down with iron. Sliding iron back and forth could result in blurred lines. Remove iron as soon as drawing is transferred. Allow paper to cool a few seconds before removing.

Step 3

Using slick paints, outline design and fill in the areas of color. You can copy the colors in the shirt photograph or paint the shirt as you wish. Red, green and glittery gold dots were painted around the neckline to decorate. Dots of crystal paint were added for snowflakes. Allow paint to dry for 4 to 6 hours before wearing shirt. Thick paint will take longer to dry.

Teddy Christmas Shirt

Materials:

❖ 1 child's sweatshirt, prewashed to remove sizing
❖ White, crystal, red, black, light brown, glittery gold, glittery silver, glittery blue and glittery green slick paints
❖ Tracing paper
❖ Black or blue fine-line iron-on transfer pen
❖ Iron

Step 1

Place tracing paper on design and use iron-on transfer pen to trace design.

Step 2

Position traced drawing (see page to left) ink side down, on front of shirt. Follow pen manufacturer's instructions for iron setting; cotton setting is usually recommended. Hold paper in place and press down with iron on drawing.

Sliding the iron back and forth could result in blurred lines. Remove iron as soon as drawing is transferred. Allow paper to cool a few seconds before removing.

Step 3

Use slick paints to outline design and fill in areas of color. You can copy the colors in the shirt photograph or paint the shirt as you wish. If you are painting on a dark-colored shirt, 2 coats of white paint will be needed to make snow.

The bear was painted white first, then light brown. Add dots of glittery blue to make the sky. Use dots of white for snow. Crystal paint will add sparkle to the snow. Allow paint to dry for 4 to 6 hours before wearing. Thick paint will take longer to dry.

A Christmas Feast

The holidays are a time for family and friends. Make that time special and prepare this Christmas menu for those gathered around your table.

Roast Turkey & Chestnut Stuffing

- ❖ 8 ounces fresh chestnuts or one 4-ounce package dried chestnuts
- ❖ 1 cup thinly sliced celery
- ❖ 1 large onion, chopped
- ❖ ½ cup butter or margarine
- ❖ 1 teaspoon dried thyme, crushed
- ❖ ¼ teaspoon pepper
- ❖ One 16-ounce loaf French or Italian bread, cut into ½-inch cubes, toasted*
- ❖ 1½ cups chicken broth
- ❖ ¼ cup water
- ❖ ¼ cup dry vermouth, sherry or chicken broth
- ❖ One 14-to-16 pound turkey
- ❖ Salt
- ❖ Cooking oil or melted butter
- ❖ Red apple wedges (optional)
- ❖ Fresh sage and/or thyme sprigs (optional)
- ❖ Cherry-Thyme Sauce (see below)

For stuffing, if using fresh chestnuts, cut an X in the flat side of each chestnut, using a small, sharp knife. Place the chestnuts in a large sauce pan and cover with cold water. Bring to a boil and reduce heat. Cover and simmer for 10 to 15 minutes. Drain. When chestnuts are cool enough to handle, peel and chop. If using dried chestnuts, cook according to package directions.

Meanwhile, in a small saucepan cook celery and onion in hot butter or margarine till tender but not brown. Stir in thyme and pepper. In a large bowl combine chestnuts and bread cubes. Stir in celery mixture. Drizzle with broth, water, and vermouth. Toss gently to coat.

Rinse turkey and pat dry. Season body cavity with salt. Spoon some stuffing loosely into neck cavity. Skewer neck skin to back. Spoon more stuffing loosely into body cavity. (If stuffing is packed too tightly it will not get hot enough by the time the turkey is done.) Tuck drumsticks under tail skin or tie to tail. Twist wing tips under the back. Transfer any remaining stuffing to a casserole; cover and chill.

Place turkey, breast side up, on a rack in a shallow roasting pan. Brush with oil or butter. Insert a meat thermometer into center of one inside thigh muscle; the thermometer bulb should not touch the bone. Cover turkey loosely with foil.

Roast turkey in a 325° oven for 4½ to 5½ hours, or until thermometer registers 180° to 185°. Cut band of skin between legs after 3½ hours. Bake casserole of stuffing alongside turkey for the last 40 to 45 minutes of cooking time. Uncover the bird for the last 30 minutes of roasting. When done, remove turkey from oven and cover. Let stand 20 minutes before carving. If desired, garnish with apple wedges and fresh sprigs of sage.

*To toast bread cubes, spread cubes in a single layer in a 15½x10½x2-inch baking pan. Bake in a 300° oven for 10 to 15 minutes or until dry, stirring twice.

Cherry-Thyme Sauce

If you like, make this sweet and savory sauce as many as three days ahead, cover and chill. Reheat sauce over medium heat, stirring gently.

- ❖ 1 cup unsweetened cherry juice
- ❖ ¾ cup chicken broth
- ❖ ½ cup dried cherries, snipped
- ❖ ¼ cup finely chopped onion
- ❖ 1 teaspoon dried thyme, crushed
- ❖ 1 teaspoon white wine Worcestershire sauce
- ❖ ½ to 1 teaspoon sugar
- ❖ ⅛ teaspoon pepper
- ❖ ¼ cup unsweetened cherry juice
- ❖ 4 teaspoons cornstarch

In a small saucepan stir together the 1 cup of cherry juice, chicken broth, dried cherries, onion, thyme, white wine Worcestershire sauce, sugar and pepper. Bring to a boil over medium-high heat; reduce heat. Cover and simmer for 15 minutes.

Stir together the ¼ cup cherry juice and cornstarch. Stir into cherry-broth mixture. Cook and stir until thickened and bubbly. Cook and stir 2 minutes longer. Serve warm with turkey. Makes 2 cups.

Swiss Corn Bake

- ❖ One 16-ounce package frozen whole kernel corn
- ❖ 2 beaten eggs
- ❖ 1½ cups (6 ounces) shredded process Swiss cheese
- ❖ Two 5-ounce cans (1¼ cups) evaporated milk
- ❖ ¼ cup finely chopped onion
- ❖ ¼ to ½ teaspoon salt
- ❖ Dash pepper
- ❖ ¾ cup (1 slice) soft whole wheat or white bread crumbs
- ❖ 2 tablespoons butter or margarine, melted
- ❖ Red sweet pepper rings (optional)
- ❖ Celery leaves (optional)

Cook corn according to package directions. Drain. In a medium mixing bowl combine eggs, the 1 cup cheese, evaporated milk, onion, salt and pepper. Stir in cooked, drained corn.

Turn mixture into an 8-inch round baking dish or a 9-inch quiche dish. Place dish on a baking sheet. Bake in a 350° oven for 20 minutes.

Toss bread crumbs with the ½ cup remaining cheese and butter or margarine. Sprinkle mixture in a ring over corn mixture. Bake 5 to 10 minutes until golden brown and bubbly. Let stand 5 minutes. If desired, top with sweet pepper rings and celery leaves. Makes 8 servings.

Colonial Green Beans and Bacon

Generations have enjoyed the smoky flavor of this vegetable and bacon dish. This year, it gets a brighter look with fresh sliced carrots.

- ❖ 7 slices bacon
- ❖ Two 9-ounce packages frozen Italian-style green beans, thawed
- ❖ 6 medium carrots, thinly sliced
- ❖ 2 tablespoons butter or margarine
- ❖ 2 cloves garlic, minced
- ❖ ½ teaspoon pepper

In a large skillet cook the bacon, uncovered, over medium heat for 8 to 10 minutes or until just crisp, turning occasionally. Remove bacon and drain on paper towels.

Drain all but 2 tablespoons of the bacon drippings from the skillet. Add green beans, carrots, butter or margarine and garlic.

Stir-fry over medium-high heat about 5 minutes or until vegetables are crisp-tender. Crumble bacon, leaving 1 strip whole for garnish, if desired. Stir crumbled bacon and pepper into vegetable mixture. Remove from heat and transfer to a serving bowl. If desired, top with reserved bacon slice. Makes 8 servings.

If you prefer a different fruit combination for this sweet-tangy salad, substitute any fresh fruit medley you want.

- ❖ ¼ cup salad oil
- ❖ ¼ cup orange juice
- ❖ 3 tablespoons balsamic vinegar
- ❖ 1 tablespoon honey
- ❖ ⅛ teaspoon cracked pepper
- ❖ 2 medium pink grapefruit
- ❖ 1 medium orange
- ❖ 2 medium pears, cored and cut into wedges
- ❖ 2 teaspoons lemon juice
- ❖ Lettuce leaves
- ❖ 1 bunch red and/or green seedless grapes

For dressing, in a blender container or food processor bowl combine salad oil, orange juice, vinegar, honey and pepper. Cover and blend or process until combined. Cover and chill until serving time.

Use a small, sharp knife to peel grapefruit and orange, removing as much of the white membranes as possible. Section grapefruit. Cut orange crosswise into 8 slices. Brush pear wedges with lemon juice.

Cover a large platter with lettuce leaves. Arrange grapefruit sections, orange slices, pear wedges, and grapes atop lettuce. Cover the platter with plastic wrap and chill for up to 4 hours. Before serving, drizzle with dressing. Makes 8 side-dish servings.

Whole Wheat Scones
with Anise

To make these moist, biscuitlike wedges ahead of time, bake them as directed and freeze for as long as three months. To serve, wrap the frozen scones in foil and reheat in a 350° oven for 15 to 20 minutes or until warm.

❖ ½ cup currants
❖ 1 cup all-purpose flour
❖ 1 cup whole wheat flour
❖ 3 tablespoons brown sugar
❖ 2 teaspoons baking powder
❖ 1 teaspoon aniseed
❖ ½ teaspoon baking soda
❖ ½ teaspoon salt
❖ ⅓ cup shortening, butter or margarine
❖ 8 ounces dairy sour cream
❖ 1 beaten egg yolk
❖ 1 slightly beaten egg white
❖ 1 teaspoon aniseed (optional)

In a small mixing bowl, pour enough hot water over currants to cover. Let stand for 5 minutes. Drain.

In a large mixing bowl, stir together both flours, brown sugar, baking powder, 1 teaspoon aniseed, baking soda and salt. Using a pastry blender, cut in shortening, butter or margarine until the mixture resembles coarse crumbs. Add currants, toss until mixed. Make a well in the center of the mixture. In a small mixing bowl combine sour cream and egg yolk. Add sour cream mixture all at once to flour mixture. Using a fork, stir just until moistened.

Turn the dough out onto a lightly floured surface. Quickly knead dough by gently folding and pressing dough for 10 to 12 strokes or until nearly smooth. Pat or lightly roll dough into a 7-inch circle. Cut into 12 wedges. Place wedges on an ungreased baking sheet in a circle, about ½ inch apart. Brush scones with egg white.

If desired, sprinkle with remaining aniseed.

Bake in a 400° oven for 10 to 12 minutes or until light brown. Cool on a wire rack for 5 minutes. Break scones into wedges if baked together. Serve warm. Makes 12 servings.

Raspberry-Sauced Cheesecakes

- ⅓ cup crushed vanilla wafers
- 2 tablespoons butter or margarine, melted
- One 8-ounce package cream cheese, softened
- ½ cup sugar
- 1 tablespoon all-purpose flour
- 1 teaspoon vanilla
- 2 eggs
- 3 tablespoons milk
- Raspberry Sauce*
- Fresh or loose-pack frozen raspberries

Grease sides and bottoms of eight 2½-inch muffin cups. For crust, stir together crushed wafers and margarine or butter. Divide mixture among muffin cups. Press onto bottoms of cups to form a firm, even crust.

For filling, beat cream cheese, sugar, flour and vanilla in a mixer bowl with an electric mixer on low speed until well combined. Add eggs all at once; beat just until combined. Stir in milk.

Pour cream cheese mixture into muffin cups. Bake in 350° oven about 20 minutes or until centers appear set. Cool. Chill 2 hours or until serving time. Loosen sides of cheesecakes with narrow spatula; remove from muffin cups. Place on dessert plates.

Spoon 1 tablespoon Raspberry Sauce over each. Top each cheesecake with several fresh or frozen raspberries. Makes 8 servings.

*Raspberry Sauce: In blender container or food processor bowl combine ½ of a 12-ounce package (1½ cups) loose-pack frozen raspberries, ¼ cup sugar, 1 teaspoon lemon juice and 1 tablespoon raspberry liqueur. Cover and blend or process until smooth. Sieve to remove seeds. Discard seeds. Makes ¾ cup.

Apricot-Nut Pudding

- 1 ¼ cups all-purpose flour
- ½ cup sugar
- 1 teaspoon baking soda
- ½ teaspoon ground cinnamon
- ¼ teaspoon ground nutmeg
- Dash ground cloves
- ¼ teaspoon salt
- ¾ cup applesauce
- ¼ cup cooking oil
- ¼ cup apple juice
- 1 beaten egg
- 1 teaspoon vanilla
- 1 cup snipped dried apricots or dried tart red cherries
- ½ cup chopped nuts
- 2 tablespoons brandy
- 2 tablespoons apple juice
- Vanilla Sauce*

Grease a 6-cup fluted tube pan; set aside. In a large mixing bowl stir together the flour, sugar, baking soda, cinnamon, nutmeg, cloves and salt. In a small mixing bowl, combine applesauce, oil, the ¼ cup apple juice, egg and vanilla. Add to flour mixture, stirring just until moist. Fold in apricots or cherries and nuts. Turn into greased pan. Grease a piece of foil and cover top of pan; seal tightly.

Bake in a 300° oven about 60 minutes or until a wooden toothpick inserted near center comes out clean. Cool in pan on rack for 10 minutes. Unmold; cool completely on rack. Place cake on rack over a pan. Combine brandy and the 2 tablespoons apple juice; drizzle evenly over pudding, tipping it to cover sides also. Wrap in plastic wrap or plastic bag. Refrigerate overnight or as long as 1 week. Serve sliced with Vanilla Sauce. Makes 10 servings.

If desired, reheat pudding before serving. Remove plastic wrap or remove from plastic bag. Wrap in foil. Heat in 325° oven for 15 to 20 minutes or until warm.

*Vanilla Sauce: In a heavy small saucepan, combine 2 slightly beaten egg yolks, 1 cup whipping cream, 3 tablespoons sugar and dash salt. Cook and stir over medium heat just until mixture is thickened and comes to a boil. Remove from heat. Pour into bowl; stir in 1 teaspoon vanilla. Cover surface with plastic wrap. Chill as long as 3 days. Makes 1⅓ cups.

Food Gifts

Laughter in the kitchen, the smell of cookies coming out of the oven, and the giving of homemade treats is all a part of Christmas. Whether you are making cookies to leave for Santa when he visits, or a special gift for a dear friend, you will find many tasty ideas on the following pages.

Maple Divinity

- 1½ cups pure maple syrup
- 1 cup sugar
- 2 egg whites
- ¼ teaspoon salt
- 1 cup broken walnuts or pecans

In a heavy 3-quart saucepan cook maple syrup and sugar. Cook over medium-high heat to boiling, stirring constantly to dissolve sugar. This should take 5 to 7 minutes. Avoid splashing mixture on sides of pan. Carefully clip candy thermometer to side of saucepan.

Cook over medium heat, without stirring, until mixture reaches 260°, hard-ball stage. Mixture should boil at a moderate, steady rate over the entire surface. Reaching hard-ball stage should take about 15 minutes.

Remove saucepan from heat; remove thermometer from saucepan. In a large mixer bowl, immediately beat egg whites and salt with a sturdy, freestanding electric mixer on medium speed until stiff peaks (tips should stand straight up).

Gradually pour hot mixture in a thin stream (slightly less than ⅛ inch diameter) over egg whites, beating with electric mixer on high speed and scraping the sides of the bowl occasionally. This should take about 3 minutes. (Add mixture *slowly* to ensure proper blending.)

Continue beating with the electric mixer on high speed, scraping the sides of the bowl occasionally, just until candy starts to lose its gloss. When beaters are lifted, mixture should fall in a ribbon, but mound on itself and not disappear into remaining mixture. Final beating should take 5 to 6 minutes.

Drop a spoonful of the mixture onto waxed paper. If it stays mounded in a soft shape, it is beaten properly. Immediately stir in nuts. Quickly drop the remaining mixture from a teaspoon onto a baking sheet lined with waxed paper. If mixture flattens, beat ½ to 1 minute more; check again. If mixture is stiff to spoon and has a rough surface, beat in hot water, a few drops at a time, until it is a softer consistency. Store tightly covered. Makes about 36 pieces.

Honey-Macadamia Nut Fudge

Toasted macadamia nuts add crunch and a wonderful flavor to this melt-in-your-mouth fudge. For a less expensive nut option, use pecans

- ❖ 1½ cups sugar
- ❖ 1 cup packed brown sugar
- ❖ ⅓ cup half-and-half or light cream
- ❖ ⅓ cup milk
- ❖ 2 tablespoons honey
- ❖ 2 tablespoons margarine or butter
- ❖ 1 teaspoon vanilla
- ❖ ½ cup toasted macadamia nuts, hazelnuts or pecans, chopped
- ❖ Chocolate-Covered Macadamia Nuts (optional)*

Prepare Chocolate-Covered Macadamia Nuts if desired; set aside. Line an 8x8x2-inch baking pan with foil, extending foil over edges of pan. Butter foil, set pan aside.

Butter sides of a heavy 2-quart saucepan. In saucepan combine sugar, brown sugar, half-and-half or cream, milk and honey. Bring to a boil over medium-high heat, stirring constantly for approximately 5 minutes with wooden spoon to dissolve sugars. Avoid splashing mixture on sides of pan. Carefully clip candy thermometer to side of pan.

Cook over medium-low heat for 10 to 12 minutes, stirring frequently, until thermometer registers 236° (softball stage). The mixture should boil at a moderate, steady rate over entire surface. Remove pan from heat. Add 2 tablespoons margarine or butter and vanilla but *do not stir*.

Cool about 50 minutes, without stirring, to lukewarm, 110°. Remove thermometer from saucepan.

With wooden spoon, beat vigorously until mixture just begins to thicken; add chopped nuts. Continue beating for approximately 10 minutes until mixture is very thick and just starts to lose its gloss. Quickly turn fudge into prepared pan. While warm, score into 1¼ inch squares.

If desired, press 1 Chocolate-Covered Macadamia nut into each square.

When firm, lift candy out of pan and cut into squares. Store in tightly covered container. Makes 36 pieces (1½ pounds).

*Chocolate-Covered Macadamia Nuts: In a small heavy saucepan, melt 4 ounces chocolate-flavored candy coating over low heat. Remove from heat. Dip 36 toasted macadamia nuts, hazelnuts or pecan halves into coating, one at a time, covering half of each nut. Let excess coating drip off. Transfer dipped nuts to waxed paper to dry. Makes 36 pieces.

Marbleized Mint Bark

Whip together this three-ingredient candy in just minutes; it's perfect for last-minute gift giving.

- ❖ ⅓ cup semisweet mint-flavored chocolate pieces or semisweet chocolate pieces
- ❖ 1 pound vanilla-flavored candy coating, cut up
- ❖ ¾ cup finely crushed candy canes or finely crushed striped round peppermint candies

Line a baking sheet with foil; set aside. In a heavy small saucepan heat chocolate pieces over low heat, stirring constantly, until melted and smooth. Remove pan from heat.

In a heavy 2-quart saucepan heat candy coating over low heat, stirring constantly, until melted and smooth. Remove pan from heat. Stir in crushed candies. Pour the melted coating mixture onto prepared baking sheet. Spread coating mixture to about a ⅜-inch thickness; drizzle with melted chocolate. Gently zigzag a narrow metal spatula through chocolate and peppermint layers to create a swirled effect.

Let candy stand several hours or until firm (candy can be chilled for 30 minutes or until firm). Use foil to lift candy from baking sheet. Carefully break into pieces. Store, lightly covered, for as long as 2 weeks. Makes about 1¼ pounds.

Black Walnut Pralines

- 1½ cups sugar
- 1½ cups packed brown sugar
- 1 cup light cream or half-and-half
- 3 tablespoons margarine or butter
- 1 cup broken black walnuts
- 1 cup raisins
- 1 teaspoon vanilla

Butter the sides of a heavy 2-quart saucepan. In saucepan, combine sugar, brown sugar and light cream or half-and-half. Cook over medium high heat to boiling, 6 to 8 minutes, stirring constantly with wooden spoon to dissolve sugar. Avoid splashing mixture on sides of pan. Carefully clip candy thermometer to side of saucepan.

Cook over medium-low heat, stirring occasionally, until thermometer registers 234°, soft-ball stage (about 16 to 18 minutes). Mixture should boil at a moderate, steady rate over entire surface.

Remove saucepan from heat. Add 3 tablespoons margarine or butter but *do not stir*. Cook, without stirring, to 150° or about 30 minutes. Remove thermometer from pan. Immediately stir in walnuts, raisins and vanilla. Beat vigorously with wooden spoon about 3 minutes, until mixture is just beginning to thicken but is still glossy. This should take 2 to 3 minutes.

Quickly drop candy from teaspoon onto baking sheet lined with waxed paper. If candy becomes too stiff to drop easily from spoon, stir in a few drops of *hot water*. Store tightly covered. Makes about 36 pralines.

Caramel Corn and Candy Crunch

Make this popcorn munch mix ahead and keep it on hand for last minute gifts or snacking.

- 7 cups popped popcorn (about ⅓ cup unpopped)
- ¾ cup packed brown sugar
- ⅓ cup butter or margarine
- 3 tablespoons light corn syrup
- ¼ teaspoon baking soda
- ¼ teaspoon vanilla
- 1 cup candy-coated milk chocolate pieces
- 1 cup peanuts
- 1 cup raisins

Remove all unpopped kernels from popped corn. Place popped corn in a greased 17x12x2-inch baking pan. Keep popcorn warm in a 300° oven while making caramel mixture.

Butter sides of a heavy 1½-quart saucepan. In saucepan combine brown sugar, butter or margarine and corn syrup. Cook over medium heat to boiling, about 7 to 10 minutes, stirring constantly with a wooden spoon to dissolve sugar. Avoid splashing mixture on sides of pan. Carefully clip candy thermometer to side of pan.

Cook over medium heat, about 4 minutes, stirring occasionally, until thermometer registers 255°, hardball stage. The mixture should boil at a moderate, steady rate over the entire surface.

Remove saucepan from heat; remove candy thermometer from saucepan. Add baking soda and vanilla; stir until well combined. Pour caramel mixture over the popcorn, stirring gently to coat popcorn. Bake in a 300° oven for 10 minutes; stir. Bake for 5 minutes more.

Turn popcorn mixture onto a large piece of foil. Cool completely. Break mixture into small pieces. Place in large bowl. Stir in candy-coated chocolate pieces, peanuts and raisins. Store in a tightly covered container. Makes 9 cups.

Hazelnut Toffee

- ¾ cup coarsely chopped hazelnuts (filberts)
- 1 cup butter
- 1¼ cups packed brown sugar
- 3 tablespoons water
- 1 tablespoon dark corn syrup
- ¾ cup milk chocolate pieces
- ¼ cup finely chopped hazelnuts (filberts)

Line a 13x9x2-inch baking pan with foil, extending foil over edges of pan. Sprinkle the ¾ cup coarsely chopped hazelnuts on the bottom of the foil-lined pan. Set pan aside.

Butter sides of heavy 2-quart saucepan. In the pan melt butter over low heat. Stir in brown sugar, water and syrup. Cook over medium-high heat to boiling, stirring constantly with a wooden spoon to dissolve sugar (for about 4 minutes). Avoid splashing mixture on sides of pan. Carefully clip candy thermometer to side of pan.

Cook over medium heat for about 15 minutes, stirring frequently, until thermometer registers 290°, soft-crack stage. Mixture should boil at a moderate, steady rate over the entire surface. Watch carefully after candy mixture reaches 280°. Remove pan from heat; remove thermometer. Immediately pour mixture into prepared pan. Let stand 2 to 3 minutes, or until surface is firm. Sprinkle with chocolate pieces; let stand 1 to 2 minutes. When softened, spread melted chocolate pieces evenly over toffee mixture.

Sprinkle with ¼ cup hazelnuts; press nuts lightly into melted chocolate. Chill until firm. Lift candy out of pan; break into pieces. Store in a tightly covered container. Makes about 48 pieces (1½ pounds).

Christmas Breakfast Wreath

- One 16-ounce package hot roll mix
- 2 tablespoons butter or margarine, melted
- ⅓ cup packed brown sugar
- 1 teaspoon ground cinnamon
- ½ cup raisins
- ½ cup chopped pecans
- 1 egg white
- 1 tablespoon water
- Powdered Sugar Icing*
- Green and red candied cherries

Prepare hot roll mix, according to package directions, through the kneading step. Let rest 5 minutes. Divide in half. Roll one portion into a 12x8-inch rectangle. Brush with half the melted butter or margarine. Stir together brown sugar and cinnamon. Sprinkle dough with half the sugar mixture, half the raisins and half the pecans.

Roll up jelly-roll-style, starting from a long side. Form into circle on greased baking sheet. Pinch ends together to seal.

Using scissors, cut dough every 1½ inches from outside almost to center. Turn each piece to lie almost flat. Repeat with remaining dough and other ingredients.

Cover and let rise in a warm place for 30 minutes or until nearly doubled in size. Beat together egg white and water; brush over breads. Bake in a 375° oven for 18 to 20 minutes or until lightly browned. Remove to wire rack, cool completely. Drizzle wreaths with Powdered Sugar Icing and decorate with candied cherries. Makes 2 wreaths, 10 servings each.

*Powdered Sugar Icing:
In a small bowl stir together 1 cup sifted powdered sugar, 1 tablespoon milk, and ¼ teaspoon vanilla. Stir in additional milk, 1 teaspoon at a time, until mixture reaches drizzling consistency. Makes about ½ cup.

Cherry-Apple Jam

- One 16-ounce package (3 cups) frozen unsweetened pitted tart red cherries
- 1 cup finely chopped apple
- ¼ cup lemon juice
- One 1¾-ounce package regular powdered fruit pectin
- 5 cups sugar

Finely chop 3 cups cherries, reserving juice. In a kettle, combine cherries and juice, apple and lemon juice. Add pectin; mix well. Bring mixture to a full rolling boil. Stir in sugar. Bring again to a full rolling boil, stirring often. Boil hard, uncovered, for 1 minute. Remove from heat. Skim off foam with metal spoon.

Ladle into hot, clean half-pint jars, leaving ¼-inch headspace. Wipe jar rims, adjust lids. Process in boiling water bath for 15 minutes. Makes 5 half-pints.

'Tis always the season to BBQ!

Plum-Good Barbecue Sauce

- ½ cup chopped onion
- 1 tablespoon margarine or butter
- One 17-ounce can purple plums
- One 6-ounce can thawed frozen lemonade concentrate

- ¼ cup catsup
- 2 tablespoons soy sauce
- 2 teaspoons prepared mustard
- 1 teaspoon ground ginger
- 1 teaspoon Worcestershire sauce

In a medium saucepan cook onion in margarine or butter until tender but not brown. Set aside. Drain plums, reserving syrup. Remove pits and discard. Place plums and syrup in blender container or food processor bowl; blend until smooth. To onion mixture in saucepan, add plum purée and all remaining ingredients. Simmer, uncovered, stirring occasionally, 10 to 15 minutes or until desired consistency is reached. Makes 3 cups.

Peach-Fig Relish

- Two 29-ounce cans peach slices
- One 5½-ounce can peach nectar
- ½ teaspoon finely shredded lemon peel

- ¼ cup lemon juice
- 1 teaspoon ground cardamom
- 3 cups chopped dried light figs
- 1 tablespoon brandy

Drain peach slices, reserving ½ cup syrup. Coarsely chop peach slices. In a large saucepan combine peaches, reserved syrup, nectar, lemon peel, lemon juice and cardamom. Bring to a boil. Reduce heat, boil gently, uncovered, for 5 minutes. Stir in figs and brandy. Cook 2 minutes more, stirring occasionally.

Ladle hot mixture into hot, clean half-pint jars, leaving a ½-inch headspace. Wipe jar rims, adjust lids. Process in a boiling water bath for 15 minutes. Makes 8 half-pints.

Cinnamon-Cranberry Vinegar

- 6 inches of stick cinnamon
- 1½ cups fresh cranberries
- 2 cups cider vinegar
- 1 cup dry red wine
- ¼ cup sugar

Place cinnamon in a clean 1-quart jar. Set aside.

In a colander, thoroughly rinse cranberries with cold water; drain well. In a stainless steel or enamel saucepan, bring cranberries, vinegar, wine and sugar to a boil; reduce heat. Boil gently, uncovered, for 3 minutes.

Pour hot cranberry mixture over cinnamon in jar. Cover jar tightly with a nonmetallic lid (or cover with plastic wrap and then tightly seal with a metal lid). Let stand in a cool, dark place for 1 week.

Line a colander with several layers of 100% cotton cheese-cloth. Strain vinegar mixture through colander and let it drain into a bowl. Discard fruit and stick cinnamon.

Transfer strained liquid to 3 clean half-pint bottles or jars. Cover bottles or jars tightly with a nonmetallic lid (or cover with plastic wrap and then tightly seal with a metal lid). Store in a cool, dark place for up to 6 months. Makes 3 half-pint jars.

Orange Streusel Muffins

- 1¾ cups all-purpose flour
- ¼ cup sugar
- 2½ teaspoons baking powder
- ½ teaspoon salt
- ¼ teaspoon finely shredded orange peel
- 1 beaten egg
- ¾ cup milk
- ⅓ cup cooking oil
- ¼ cup orange marmalade
- 2 teaspoons finely chopped pecans
- 2 tablespoons sugar
- ¼ teaspoon ground cinnamon

Grease thirty-six 1¾-inch (or twelve 2½-inch) muffin cups or line with paper baking cups. Set aside.

For batter, in a medium mixing bowl stir together flour, the ¼ cup sugar, baking powder, salt and orange peel. Make a well in the center.

In a small mixing bowl combine egg, milk and oil. Add egg mixture all at once to flour mixture. Stir until moistened. Batter should be slightly lumpy.

Spoon a rounded teaspoon of the batter into each prepared cup for 1¾-inch muffins (use 1 tablespoon for 2½-inch muffins). Top each with about ½ teaspoon of marmalade for 1¾-inch muffins (use about 1 teaspoon for 2½-inch muffins).

Spoon another rounded teaspoon of batter on top of marmalade in each cup for 1¾-inch muffins (use about 1 tablespoon for 2½-inch muffins). Sprinkle with nuts and a mixture of 2 tablespoons sugar and cinnamon.

Bake in a 400° oven for 15 to 18 minutes (20 to 25 minutes for 2½-inch muffins) or until golden. Remove muffins from muffin cups and cool on wire racks. Makes thirty-six 1¾-inch muffins or twelve 2½-inch muffins.

To make ahead: Prepare Orange Streusel Muffins as directed above. Wrap muffins tightly in heavy foil or place them in freezer bags. They can be frozen for as long as 3 months. Thaw wrapped muffins at room temperature for about 30 minutes.

Cranberry Crescents

- 6 cups all-purpose flour
- 1 envelope active dry yeast
- ¼ teaspoon salt
- 2 cups margarine or butter
- 3 egg yolks
- One 8-ounce carton dairy sour cream
- 2 teaspoons vanilla
- Cranberry-Prune Filling*
- Sour Cream Icing*

Combine flour, yeast and salt. Cut in margarine or butter until mixture resembles coarse crumbs. Combine egg yolks, sour cream and vanilla. Add to flour mixture. Stir or knead to form a smooth ball. Divide into 8 portions. Cover and chill.

Sprinkle work surface with powdered sugar. Roll each dough portion into an 8-inch circle. Cut into 8 wedges. Place 1 slightly rounded teaspoon of Cranberry-Prune Filling near the wide end of each wedge. Roll up, starting with the wide end. Place, point side down, on an ungreased baking sheet. Curve slightly to form crescents. Bake in 350° oven for 18 to 20 minutes or until golden. Cool on a wire rack. While warm, drizzle with Sour Cream Icing. Makes 64 crescents.

*Cranberry-Prune Filling: Cook one 12-ounce bag of cranberries and 1 cup sugar, covered, over low heat just until mixture starts to form juice. Boil gently, uncovered, for 5 minutes or until berries pop.

Stir in one 12-ounce package of dried pitted prunes, finely snipped, ¼ cup light raisins, ¼ cup chopped walnuts, 1 ½ teaspoons finely shredded lemon peel and 1 tablespoon lemon juice. Cool, cover and chill.

*Sour Cream Icing: Combine ½ cup dairy sour cream and ½ teaspoon vanilla. Stir in 1 to 1¼ cups sifted powdered sugar to make icing of drizzling consistency.

Carrot Marmalade

- 1 orange
- 2 or 3 lemons
- 1¼ cups water
- 1½ pounds carrots, cut up
- 7 cups sugar
- 1 pouch liquid fruit pectin

Cut up orange and one lemon; discard seeds. In food processor, finely chop fruit. Place in medium saucepan. Squeeze remaining lemons and measure ¼ cup juice; add juice to fruit. Add water. Bring to a boil; reduce heat. Cover and simmer 20 minutes, stirring occasionally.

In a food processor, coarsely shred about 5 cups carrots. Add to orange mixture. Measure 4½ cups of the carrot marmalade mixture into 6- or 8-quart Dutch oven. Stir in sugar. Bring to a full, rolling boil, stirring constantly. Quickly stir in pectin.

Return to full, rolling boil, stirring constantly. Boil hard 1 minute, stirring. Remove from heat. Skim off foam. Ladle into clean, hot jars, leaving ¼-inch headspace. Adjust lids. Process in boiling water bath for 15 minutes. Makes 8 half-pints.

Papaya-Apple Chutney

- 2 medium tart cooking apples, peeled, cored and chopped
- 1 medium papaya (1½ cups), seeded, peeled and chopped
- ½ cup packed brown sugar
- ⅓ cup chopped green pepper
- ⅓ cup vinegar
- ¼ cup water
- 2 tablespoons chopped onion
- 1 tablespoon lime or lemon juice
- ¼ teaspoon salt
- 1 clove garlic, minced
- ¼ cup slivered, toasted almonds

In a large saucepan, combine all ingredients except almonds. Bring to a boil; reduce heat. Simmer 30 minutes, stirring occasionally. Cool, cover and store in refrigerator as long as 4 weeks. Chutney can be frozen for as long as 12 months. Before serving, stir in almonds. Makes about 2¼ cups.

Tex-Mex Cheese Crisps

- ❖ 1½ cups (6 ounces) shredded cheddar cheese
- ❖ ¾ cup margarine or butter
- ❖ 1 egg
- ❖ 1 to 1½ teaspoons chili powder
- ❖ ¼ teaspoon ground red pepper
- ❖ ⅛ teaspoon garlic powder
- ❖ ⅛ teaspoon salt (optional)
- ❖ 1¾ cups all-purpose flour

Allow margarine or butter and cheese to come to room temperature. In a mixing bowl beat cheese and margarine or butter together. Add egg, chili powder, ground red pepper, garlic powder and salt, if desired. Beat well. Stir in flour until well combined, kneading the last of the flour by hand if necessary.

Using a cookie press, press dough onto an ungreased baking sheet. If using a ribbon plate, pipe strips and cut every 2 inches. Bake in a 375° oven for 8 to 10 minutes or until lightly browned. Remove from baking sheet immediately to a wire rack and cool. Store in an airtight container in the refrigerator or freezer. Makes 70 to 80.

Twist-O-Caraway Sticks

- ❖ 1 beaten egg
- ❖ 1 tablespoon water
- ❖ 1 teaspoon country-style Dijon mustard or prepared mustard
- ❖ ¾ cup (3 ounces) shredded Swiss cheese
- ❖ ¼ cup finely chopped onion
- ❖ 2 teaspoons snipped parsley
- ❖ 1½ teaspoons caraway seed
- ❖ ¼ teaspoon garlic salt
- ❖ ½ of a 17¼-ounce package frozen puff pastry (1 sheet), thawed

In a small bowl combine egg, water and mustard, set aside. In a medium bowl stir together cheese, onion, parsley, caraway seed and garlic salt. Unfold pastry sheet. Brush generously with egg mixture. Sprinkle cheese mixture lengthwise over half of the rectangle. Fold plain half over cheese, lining up edges and pressing to seal.

Brush top of pastry with egg mixture. With a sharp knife, cut pastry crosswise into ½-inch-wide strips. Twist each strip several times and place 1 inch apart on greased baking sheet, pressing ends down. Bake in a 350° oven for 18 to 20 minutes or until light brown. Serve warm. Makes about 18.

Hot Pepper Pecans

- ❖ 2 tablespoons margarine or butter
- ❖ 1 cup large pecan halves
- ❖ 2 teaspoons soy sauce
- ❖ ¼ teaspoon bottled hot pepper sauce

Melt margarine or butter in an 8x8x2-inch baking pan. Spread nuts in pan. Bake in a 300° oven for 30 minutes, stirring often.

Combine soy and pepper sauces; stir into nuts. Spread onto paper towel until cool. Store in a jar. Makes 1 cup.

Mustard-Marinated Mushrooms

- ❖ ⅓ cup Dijon-style mustard
- ❖ ⅓ cup wine vinegar
- ❖ ¾ teaspoon dried oregano, crushed
- ❖ ½ teaspoon dried tarragon, crushed
- ❖ ½ teaspoon salt
- ❖ ¼ teaspoon pepper
- ❖ ⅔ cup olive or salad oil
- ❖ 16 ounces (6 cups) fresh mushrooms, sliced
- ❖ ⅔ cup pitted ripe olives, halved crosswise

In a large mixing bowl combine mustard, vinegar, oregano, tarragon, salt and pepper. Using a wire whisk, blend in oil. Stir in mushrooms and olives. Cover and chill at least 2 hours, stirring occasionally. Store in refrigerator as long as 1 week. Makes 4 cups.

Savory Pepper Spread

- ❖ 4 red or green sweet peppers
- ❖ ¼ cup pitted ripe olives
- ❖ 2 tablespoons balsamic vinegar or cider vinegar
- ❖ 1 teaspoon sugar
- ❖ ¼ teaspoon salt
- ❖ 1 tablespoon margarine or butter
- ❖ 1 teaspoon snipped fresh parsley

To roast peppers, quarter them and remove stems, seeds and membranes. Place, cut side down, on a foil-lined baking sheet. Bake in a 425° oven for 20 to 25 minutes or until skins are bubbly and browned. Remove from baking sheet and place in a new brown paper bag.

Close bag and let stand about 30 minutes to steam so the skin peels away easily. Pull the skin off gently and slowly, using a paring knife.

In a food processor bowl or blender container, add roasted peppers, olives, vinegar, sugar and salt. Cover and process or blend until smooth. Pour into a medium saucepan.

Add margarine or butter. Bring to a boil. Reduce heat; cook and stir over medium-low heat for 10 minutes or until excess liquid is evaporated. Remove from heat. Stir in parsley; cool. Turn into a storage container. Cover; chill as long as 3 weeks. Makes 1 cup.

Orange Praline Sauce

- ½ cup sugar
- ½ cup packed brown sugar
- 2 tablespoons all-purpose flour
- Dash salt
- 1 teaspoon finely shredded orange peel
- ⅓ cup orange juice
- ⅔ cup water
- ½ cup miniature marshmallows
- 2 tablespoons margarine or butter
- ½ cup broken pecans
- 1 teaspoon vanilla

In a saucepan, stir together sugars, flour and salt. Stir in orange peel, orange juice and water. Cook and stir over medium heat until thickened and bubbly. Add marshmallows and margarine or butter.

Cook and stir until marshmallows and margarine or butter are melted. Remove from heat; add pecans and vanilla. Serve warm over ice cream. Pour sauce into jars. Makes 2 cups.

To reheat, cook and stir in a medium saucepan over low heat until warm. Or, in a microwave-safe glass measure micro-cook on 100% power (high) 30 to 60 seconds or until warm.

Chocolate Hazelnut Sauce

- 3 squares (3 ounces) semisweet chocolate, cut up
- ¼ cup margarine or butter
- One 5-ounce can evaporated milk
- ½ cup sugar
- 3 tablespoons hazelnut liqueur

In a heavy, small saucepan melt chocolate and butter or margarine over low heat, stirring frequently. Add evaporated milk and sugar. Cook and stir over medium heat for about 5 minutes or until mixture is slightly thickened and bubbly.

Remove from heat. Add liqueur and stir until smooth. Cool slightly. Serve warm over ice cream. Pour sauce into jars. Cover and chill as long as 1 month. Makes 1½ cups.

To reheat, cook and stir in a medium saucepan over low heat until warm. Or, in a microwave-safe glass measure micro-cook on 100% power (high) 30 to 60 seconds or until warm.

Chocolate Pinwheels

- Two 11-ounce packages pie crust mix
- ¾ cup milk chocolate pieces, melted and cooled
- 2 tablespoons sugar
- Sugar

In medium bowl finely crumble two pie crust sticks. Stir in chocolate. Using your hands, make it into a smooth dough. Divide in half. Crumble remaining 2 pie crust sticks into medium bowl. Stir in 2 tablespoons sugar. With fork, stir in ¼ cup warm water until moistened.

Divide dough in half. On lightly floured surface, roll each half of plain dough to an 8x8-inch square. Roll each chocolate portion to an 8x8-inch square. Place one plain square on top of chocolate square. Roll up each jelly-roll-style and seal each edge. Roll dough in sugar. Wrap and chill in freezer 20 minutes or in refrigerator 1 hour.

Slice dough into ¼-inch slices and place on ungreased cookie sheet. Bake in 375° oven for 12 minutes or until edges are set. Cool on wire rack. Makes about 60 cookies.

Big Soft Ginger Cookies

- 2¼ cups all-purpose flour
- 2 teaspoons ground ginger
- 1 teaspoon baking soda
- ¾ teaspoon ground cinnamon
- ½ teaspoon ground cloves
- ¼ teaspoon salt
- ¾ cup margarine, butter or shortening
- 1 cup sugar
- 1 egg
- ¼ cup molasses
- 2 tablespoons sugar

Combine flour, ginger, soda, cinnamon, cloves and salt. Set aside.

In a large mixing bowl beat margarine, butter or shortening with an electric mixer on low speed for 30 seconds to soften. Gradually add the 1 cup sugar and beat until fluffy. Add egg and molasses; beat well. Beat or stir in flour mixture.

Shape into 1½-inch balls (1 heaping tablespoon dough each). Roll in the 2 tablespoons sugar and place about 2½ inches apart on an ungreased cookie sheet.

Bake in a 350° oven for 10 minutes or until edges are set and cookies are still puffed (do not over-bake). Let stand for 2 minutes before transferring to a wire rack. Cool. Makes 24 cookies.

Mocha Truffle Cookies

- ½ cup margarine or butter
- ½ cup semisweet chocolate pieces
- 1 tablespoon instant coffee crystals
- ¾ cup sugar
- ¾ cup packed brown sugar
- 2 eggs
- 2 teaspoons vanilla
- 2 cups all-purpose flour
- ⅓ cup unsweetened cocoa powder
- ½ teaspoon baking powder
- ¼ teaspoon salt
- 1 cup semisweet chocolate pieces

In a large saucepan melt margarine or butter and the ½ cup chocolate pieces over low heat. Remove from heat. Stir in coffee crystals and cool 5 minutes. Stir in sugars, eggs and vanilla. In a medium mixing bowl combine flour, cocoa powder, baking powder and salt. Stir into coffee mixture. Stir in the 1 cup chocolate pieces. Drop dough by rounded tablespoon onto lightly greased cookie sheets. Bake in a 350° oven for 10 minutes. Let cool 1 minute before removing from sheet. Makes 30 cookies.

Cranberry-Pecan Tassies

- ½ cup butter or margarine
- One 3-ounce package cream cheese, softened
- 1 cup all-purpose flour
- 1 egg
- ¾ cup packed brown sugar
- 1 tablespoon margarine or butter, melted
- 1 teaspoon finely shredded orange peel
- ½ cup chopped cranberries
- ½ cup chopped pecans

Beat together the ½ cup butter or margarine and cream cheese. Stir in flour and mix well. Cover and chill for 1 hour.

For filling, stir together egg, brown sugar, the 1 tablespoon melted butter or margarine and orange peel in a small bowl until smooth. Stir in cranberries and pecans; set aside. Shape chilled dough into 24 1-inch balls. Place each ball in an ungreased 1¾-inch muffin cup. Press dough onto bottom and sides of cups.

Spoon about 1 tablespoon filling into each cup, stirring filling occasionally. Bake in 325° oven for 25 to 30 minutes or until filling is set. Cool and remove from pans. Store, tightly covered in the refrigerator. Makes 24 tassies.

Licorice Caramels

Looking for a mild, unbeliev-
ably delicious licorice flavor?
You'll find black and red
paste for coloring these
candies in specialty and cake
decorating stores.

❖ 1 cup butter
   (do not use margarine)
❖ 2 cups sugar
❖ One 14-ounce can
   (1¼ cups) sweetened
   condensed milk
❖ 1 cup light corn syrup
❖ ⅛ teaspoon salt
❖ 1 teaspoon anise extract
❖ ½ teaspoon black or red
   coloring paste

To wrap caramels: Tear off
6-inch strips of waxed paper.
Cut each strip into 4-inch
widths, making 6x4-inch
pieces. Roll caramel in length
of paper and fold flaps under.
Set caramels into gift boxes
with flaps underneath. The
caramels pack neatly and stay
tightly wrapped.

Line a 9x9x2-inch baking pan
with foil, extending foil over
edges of pan. Butter foil and
set aside.

In a heavy 3-quart saucepan
melt butter over low heat.
Add sugar, sweetened
condensed milk, corn syrup
and salt; mix well. Heat over
low heat, stirring constantly,
until melted and smooth.
Carefully clip a candy
thermometer to side of pan.

Cook over medium heat, 15 to
20 minutes, stirring frequently,
until candy thermometer
registers 244 °, firm ball stage.
The mixture should boil at
moderate, steady rate over
entire surface. The mixture
scorches easily. Remove from
heat; remove candy thermometer from saucepan.
Add anise extract and
coloring; stir to mix.

Quickly pour candy, without
scraping, into buttered-foil-
lined pan. Cool for several
hours or until firm. Use foil to
lift candy out of pan onto
cutting board. Peel foil away
and discard. With a buttered
sharp knife cut into 1-inch
squares. Wrap individually in
waxed paper. Makes 64 pieces
(2¾ pounds).

Ribbons and Bows

Glossary of Ribbon Terms

ANTIQUE: Authentic or reproduction ribbons from past centuries.

BROCADE: Heavyweight silk or woven, figured, or floral ribbon; in some instances metallic threads are incorporated.

CHIFFON: Exceedingly fine-textured, soft, lightweight taffeta.

GROSGRAIN: Ribbon of ribbed fabric with the heaviest thread running crosswise.

IRIDESCENT: The weave of a ribbon that gives a rainbow effect; as the ribbon is moved, the colors of the prism appear.

JACQUARD: The weave of a ribbon that gives an intricate, variegated pattern.

MOIRÉ: The weave of a ribbon that creates a water effect.

MOTIF: The units of a design that are repeated in a pattern.

OMBRÉ: The weave of a ribbon that gives a shaded effect.

ORGANDY: A soft, thin, transparent ribbon of silk, cotton or rayon.

SATIN: Silk with a close weave, resulting in a glossy, rich effect.

TAFFETA: An extremely fine-textured, smooth silk that is one of the oldest weaves.

VELVET: Silk that is often woven on a cotton back with thick pile.

WIRED: Ribbon woven with wire edges (the wire is treated as a thread when weaving) that is used to hold a shape for bows and twists.

Single Bow

Instructions for single bow will make a single bow with an overall width of 5¹/₂ inches with two 4¹/₂-inch long streamers.

Step 1

Cut one yard of ribbon into one 20-inch piece to use for loops and one 16-inch piece to use for streamers.

Step 2

Using the 20-inch length, form a loop of desired fullness with ribbon held firmly between thumb and index finger (see illustration 1).

Step 3

Holding bow center, twist ribbon and form a second loop opposite the first.

Secure center with a twist of wire (see illustration 2).

Ribbon loop ends will be trimmed after streamers are added.

Step 4

To make bow streamers, tie remaining ribbon length around bow center (see illustrations 3 and 4). Trim away ribbon loop ends.

Trim bow streamers to desired length and shape (see illustration 5).

illustration 5

illustration 2

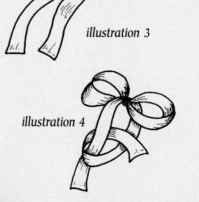

illustration 3

illustration 4

illustration 1

Double/Fuller Bows

Follow the steps for creating a single bow, making the length used for bow loops twice as long for a double bow, or three times as long for a triple bow. After second bow loop is formed, twist ribbon to form a loop on top of the first loop. Working from side to side, twist and loop ribbon until a bow of desired fullness is formed. Secure center with a twist of wire.

Ladder Bow

A variation of a decorative bow used in Victorian millinery, this chain of single bows is both great fun to tie and useful to adorn basket handles and glue to barrettes. Ladder bows are quite pretty to wear with French-braided hair. These instructions will make a ladder bow 3 inches wide overall and 4 inches long.

Step 1

Cut one 3-yard length of ribbon.

Step 2

First bow should be tied at center point of ribbon length (see illustrations 6, 7 and 8).

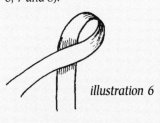

illustration 6

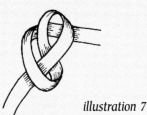

illustration 7

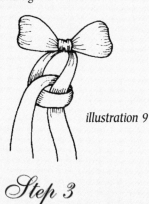

illustration 8

Tie a single knot after each bow (see illustration 9). After tying knot, adjust bow loops and tighten knot.

illustration 9

Step 3

Tie another single bow, a knot, and continue with this pattern of bows and knots until the needed length of bow chain is formed (see illustration 10).

Step 4

Trim streamers to the desired length.

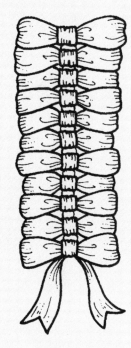

illustration 10

Acknowledgements

A heartfelt thank-you to the many people who helped the editor in creating this book. We express our gratitude to the designers who created projects expressly for this book, to the photographers and photostylists for their creative contributions, to the companies who generously shared their expertise and products with us, and to all who contributed in any way to the production of *Christmas at Home* book, especially to Tancredi & Morgen of Carmel Valley, CA, for the loan of wonderful photography props.

Design Credits

Laura Conrad—
page 37

Country Threads—
pages 28, 29, 30, 32

Craftways—
pages 15, 46, 60, 68, 69

Phyllis Dunstan—
pages 42, 81

Pam Dyer—
pages 24, 48

Hope Eastman—
page 16

Dixie Falls—
page 91

Donna Haynes—
page 8

Linda Hebert—
page 52

Gail Kinkead—
page 20

Joni Prittie—
pages 8, 10, 11, 12, 17, 18, 40, 58, 63, 64, 71, 73, 77, 78, 80, 82, 85, 94, 95, 96, 102, 105, 106, 108, 109, 110, 112, 113, 114, 115, 116, 119

Nancy Reames—
page 49

Joan Risney—
page 65

Jodee Risney—
pages 23, 39, 55, 67, 87, 97, 99, 100, 101, 102

Valerie Root—
page 26

Bonnie Wedge—
page 56

Resource Guide

B & B Kiwi Designs
3684 Larkin Road
Biggs, CA 95917

Bell'ochio
8 Brady Street
San Francisco, CA 94103

Binnie & Smith
Consumer Information
1100 Church Street
P.O. Box 431
Easton, PA 18004

**D. Blumchen
& Company**
P.O. Box 929
Maywood, NJ 07607

The Dalee Book Company
267 Douglass Street
Brooklyn, NY 11217

Design Originals
2425 Cullen Street
Fort Worth, TX 76107

Duncan Enterprises
5673 E. Shields Avenue
Fresno, CA 93727

Elsie's Exquisiques
208 State Street
P.O. Box 260
St. Joseph, MI 49085

The Gifted Line
700 Larkspur Landing Circle
Suite 163
Larkspur, CA 94939

JHB International
Denver, CO 80231

Paulette Knight
343 Vermont Street
San Francisco, CA 94102

**Lion Ribbon
Company, Inc.**
100 Metro Way
P.O. Box 1548
Secaucus, NJ 07096

Matthew Thomas Designs
8868 Clairemont Mesa Blvd.
Suite A
San Diego, CA 92123

MPR Associates, Inc.
P.O. Box 7343
High Point, NC 27264

Naturally Yours
1423 Buckskin Drive
Santa Maria, CA 93454

Sulky of America
3113-D Broadpoint Drive
Harbor Heights, FL 33983

Westpoint Pepperell
Mission Valley Plant
P.O. Box 311807
New Braunfels, TX 78131-
1807

Index

Crafts

Food

If you would like to order
any additional copies of our
books, call 1-800-678-2802
or check with your local
bookstore.